Triumphs and Tragedies

Corregidor and Its Aftermath

Triumphs And Tragedies

Corregidor And Its Aftermath

Arthur B. Baker
as told to J. Carlile Baker

Essence
PUBLISHING
Belleville, Ontario, Canada

TRIUMPHS AND TRAGEDIES

National Library of Canada Cataloguing in Publication

Baker, Arthur B., 1918-

Triumphs and tragedies : Corregidor and its aftermath / Arthur B. Baker ; as told to J. Carlile Baker.

Includes bibliographical references.

ISBN 1-55306-703-7.--ISBN 1-55306-705-3 (LSI ed.)

1. Baker, Arthur B., 1918- 2. World War, 1939-1945--Prisoners and prisons, Japanese. 3. World War, 1939-1945--Personal narratives, American. 4. Prisoners of war--Japan--Biography. 5. Prisoners of war--United States--Biography. I. Baker, J. Carlile II. Title.

D805.J3B34 2004 940.54'7252'092 C2004-900189-2

Essence Publishing is a Christian Book Publisher dedicated to furthering the work of Christ through the written word. For more information, contact:

20 Hanna Court, Belleville, Ontario, Canada K8P 5J2.
Phone: 1-800-238-6376 • Fax: (613) 962-3055.
E-mail: publishing@essencegroup.com
Internet: www.essencegroup.com

Table of Contents

Acknowledgments

FIRST OF ALL, I MUST THANK DR. GOODALL, WHO EXAMINED me on May 22, 2000. She had read a considerable portion of my medical history. We talked at length concerning my WWII experience. She thanked me for my service to America, and then encouraged me to tell my story. Dr. Goodall is one of those special people who have touched my life over the years.

Then I must tell you how much I appreciate my son and daughter-in-law, Art and Jane Baker. They are the ones who have worked so very hard to put this story into book form. We talked—they worked. We talked—they worked some more. They are jewels, and I love them very much.

Then I must love my wife of fifty-six years, Geneva, even more. She was the one who went with me through that dark period—commonly known as post-traumatic stress—of my life after the war. That portion of my life I had managed for the most part to put aside; however, those dark days of memory returned during January and

February 2001, as I began *Triumphs and Tragedies,* and they were a little hard to endure. As always, Neva was there to comfort me, even as I chose to return in memory to that valley of atrocity and death. God sent Neva into my life, and I love her very, very much.

Finally, I must say how thankful I am to be an American. America is still the best place on earth to live. If you believe otherwise, I encourage you to live with the average people in the land of your dreams for a while. It will not take long to convince you that America is a great nation. With this story, I hope to convince all Americans that our country is worth fighting for.

Foreword

ARTHUR BAKER TELLS HIS STORY AS PART OF THE VALIANT battle for Corregidor in the opening months of World War II in the Pacific—his capture and enslavement as a laborer for Japanese companies from 1942–45, his determination to survive, and the joyous moment of his return to his Texas hometown—with a candor and humor which give his narrative great force. This is not a book that the reader puts down easily, because it reminds us all of how brutal the Japanese government and its corporations were to our prisoners of war, and their stubbornly unpaid debt to the survivors and their families. The Japanese government ordered its corporations to pay our POWs a specific amount, and Mitsui Mining Co. still owes Baker his back wages.

Compounding the anguish for Baker's family was the fact that, for over a year, the Japanese government refused to cooperate with the Red Cross. Lists of Allied prisoners, their whereabouts, and death certificates were withheld, making it impossible in most cases for our government to confirm that these men were still alive as POWs. Yet, the Japanese were so precise with internal information about our prisoners that they delivered mail and Red Cross packages to exactly the right camps for each prisoner—but refused to distribute them. So, Baker and his fellow POWs did not receive medicines, clothing, and food that were locked in company warehouses throughout the war. Such egregious policy was a large factor in the chilling statistic that nine out of ten POWs who died during World War II perished in Japanese, not Nazi custody. The death rate in Japanese POW camps averaged forty percent, while in Nazi military POW camps, it was just over one percent.

How close Baker came—many times—to being one of those statistics is told in a straightforward way that makes the reader marvel anew at the bravery and determination of those who truly are our "greatest generation." An Australian general, reflecting on the experience of men held prisoner by the Japanese, remarked: "When death was preferable, these men dared to live." That, in itself, is a daily act of heroism.

In researching and interviewing Pacific POWs over the last two decades, this historian has been struck by how many were Texans like Baker. These young men were among the first to answer their country's call to service, both prior to and after the war erupted at Pearl Harbor in the closing days of 1941. We owe them so much, and Baker's story inspires us anew to remember what sacrifice, and the triumph which can emerge from tragedy, are all about.

Linda Goetz Holmes
Shelter Island, New York
September 2002

Linda Goetz Holmes, a Pacific War historian, is the author of *Unjust Enrichment: How Japan's Companies Built Postwar Fortunes Using American POWs* (2001), and *4000 Bowls of Rice: a Prisoner of War Comes Home* (1994).

Preface

AMERICA FACES A TIME AS THIS CENTURY BEGINS WHEN OUR enemy brings war to our shores. For the first time in five generations, we suffer the mass destruction of our own people and property on our own soil.

My daughter-in-law asked me, "When is it all right to go to war?" My answer: "When the enemy attacks your territory and threatens those you love, you have the right, the responsibility to go to war." Extremist Muslim terrorists have clearly brought war to New York City, the Pentagon, and Pennsylvania. It appears they will in time attempt to bring war to the rest of our nation.

My purpose as I write is to encourage our young people to learn to think and act in ways that will protect us from the loss of our freedom, our democracy, our capitalism, our way of life—whatever enemy we face.

I had no idea when we began working on *Triumphs and Tragedies* that the hate of WWII would revisit us on September 11, 2001. Nor did I realize I would have the opportunity to share my insight with those unaccustomed to such brutality and inhumanity.

Anyone who has gone through tragic times knows that it is easiest to force remembrance into the back of your mind and push on with the rest of your life. Why now, in the golden years of my life, would I deliberately reflect on the horrors of my POW experience during World War II? I'm hoping that I might help those younger than I to move away from the currently fashionable question, "What's in it for me?" That question won't maintain our freedom. I suggest a view of the things necessary to see you through whatever is to come, as we face the Holy War of Osama Bin Laden and his kin, or any other extreme conflict.

Today, as we did at the outset of World War II, we need Americans to step forward for the good of America. Many have already taken steps in New York City and across the nation. The response of the country, whether from the people of New York City or those donating blood and money in all fifty states, has been heartwarming. The good people of New York stepped forward, recognizing they have little choice but to face the horrific truth that they are a hated target. As did the soldiers of WWII, they and we have one option for survival: face death, massive destruction, and crushing changes to our lives with every resource and every strategy required to survive and turn back an unimaginable enemy.

The enemy wants us to believe he's too terrible to face. In fact, our only chance of survival requires that we face him. There are more battles to fight, however, than over the twin towers of the World Trade Center. One is at the very center of our selves.

Several people who know parts of my story have said I should tell it all. With *Triumphs and Tragedies,* I hope I've met that request. I want to make it clear that this is not the story of a hero, or of the heroes I knew. It's a story of ordinary men and women who experienced extraordinary events with the philosophy that freedom is worth fighting for. It's the story of ordinary people—some who loved God, some who didn't, but whom God loved—and how we got through a time when we were treated like animals. It's the story of what it takes to face the unimaginable when you have no choice, and the constant presence of God, no matter what our circumstances—even during war, torture, and imprisonment.

Please allow me a comment. America has always claimed to stand upon the foundation of faith in God. Lately, though, we seem to slide further and further away from Him toward dependence upon ourselves. Our definition of separation of church and state is now a far cry from what our forefathers envisioned. They hoped our constitution would prevent government from ramming any certain brand of faith down the collective throats of our people, yet now it seems faithlessness is the constitutionally protected standard of the day, considered politically correct. In our day, those who would express faith in something other than themselves are hushed.

Until the events of September 11, 2001, many Americans were content to trust our own intellects as the final say in everything, our own hearts as the final conscience. Following that infamous day, many people have returned to churches, synagogues, and mosques looking for sense in a senseless situation—at least suspecting that the only One with true answers, whatever we face, is God.

I believe the "me first" generation of my children may have been replaced by the "me only" generation of my grandchildren. Both need to know about common-sense decisions made by what is called the Great Generation by some: the Americans who fought in WWII and those who supported them. The lessons of WWII are timeless, yet contemporary. Men and women who are young and strong will need these lessons to keep this country strong. My buddies and I learned two extremely important truths that work at any time, but especially in war. First, *assess your options*—then, *use what you have*. Second, the overriding theme of my life in the South Pacific theatre was a *positive attitude*. A positive attitude is helpful in peaceful times, but it is crucial, even lifesaving, in war. I keep a positive attitude even today. It still works for this old soldier. With the hope that as you read, you will be strengthened to face whatever is coming, here is my story.

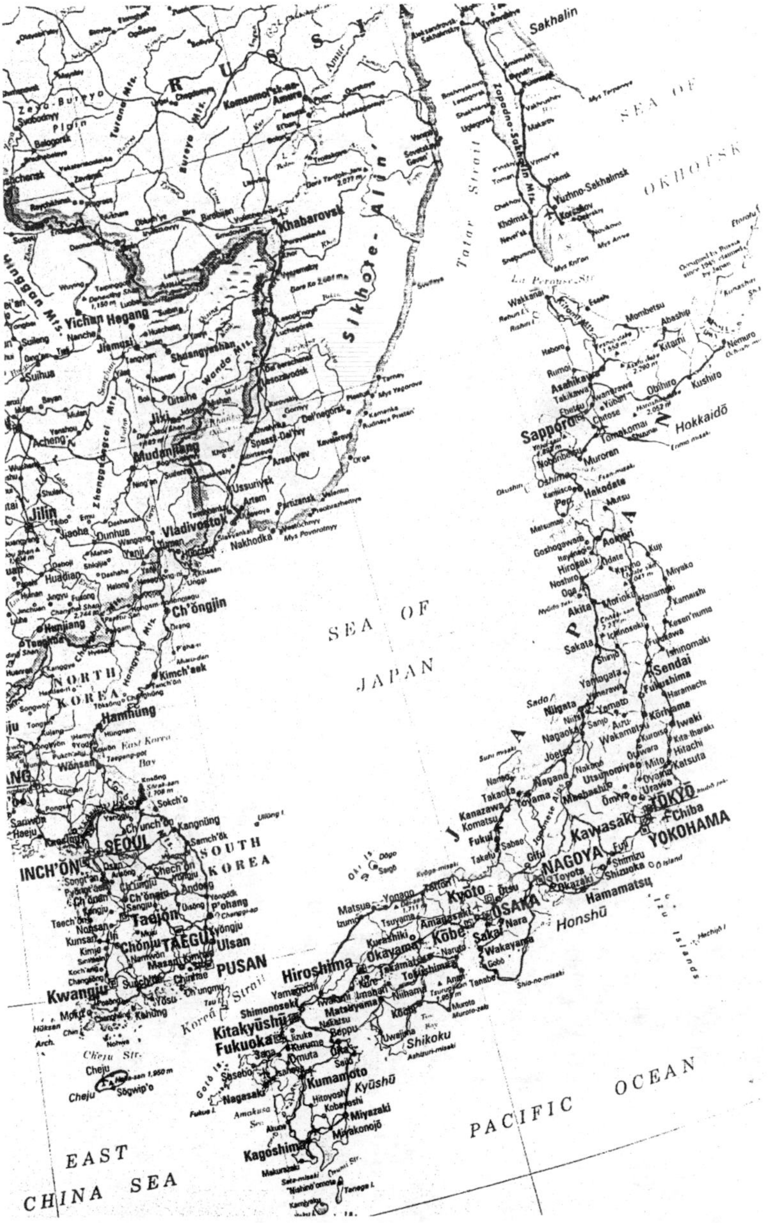
RUSSIA
Sakhalin
SEA OF OKHOTSK
Tatar Strait
Sikhote-Alin
Khabarovsk
Vladivostok
Nakhodka
Yuzhno-Sakhalinsk
La Perouse Str.
Hokkaidō
Sapporo
Hakodate
Aomori
Sendai
SEA OF JAPAN
JAPAN
NORTH KOREA
Ch'ŏngjin
Hamhŭng
East Korea Bay
SEOUL
INCH'ŎN
SOUTH KOREA
Taejŏn
TAEGU
PUSAN
Kwangju
Korea Strait
Cheju Str.
Cheju
Hiroshima
Kitakyūshū
Fukuoka
Nagasaki
Kumamoto
Kyūshū
Kagoshima
Shikoku
Okayama
Kobe
OSAKA
Kyoto
NAGOYA
Honshū
TŌKYŌ
YOKOHAMA
Kawasaki
Niigata
Hamamatsu
PACIFIC OCEAN
EAST CHINA SEA

11-8-32-9A 12-2000 FT.

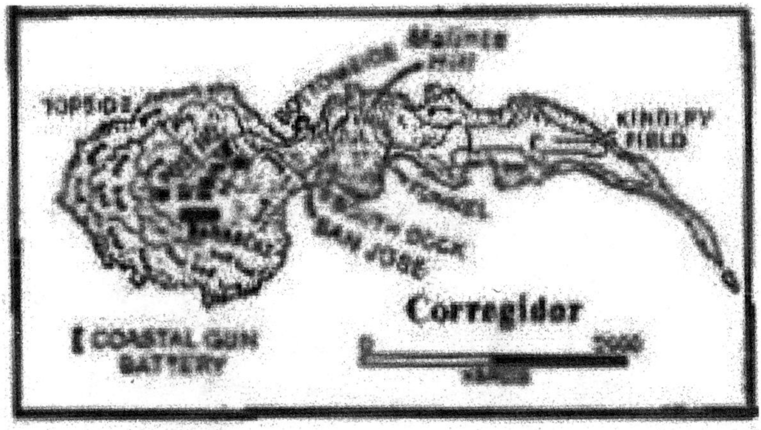
TOPSIDE
SAN JOSE
Corregidor
COASTAL GUN
BATTERY

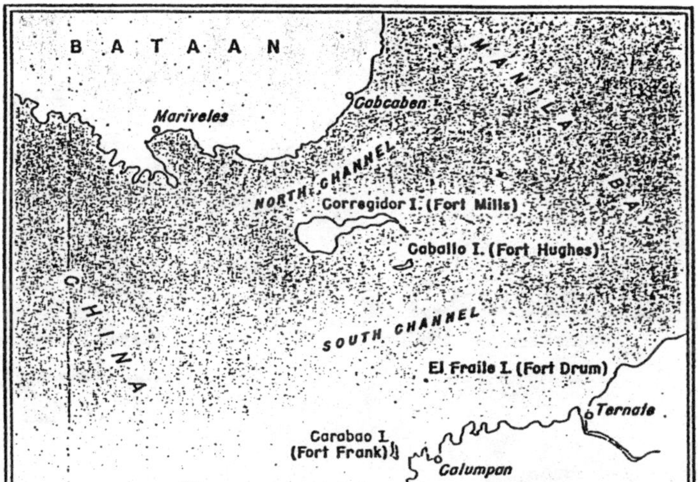
B A T A A N
MANILA BAY
Cabcaben
Mariveles
NORTH CHANNEL
Corregidor I. (Fort Mills)
Caballo I. (Fort Hughes)
CHINA
SOUTH CHANNEL
El Fraile I. (Fort Drum)
Ternate
Carabao I.
(Fort Frank)
Calumpan
SEA
PICO DE LORO
HILLS
CAVITE
BATANGAS
0
5
MILES

LUZON
Subic Bay
OLONGAPO
HERMOSA
FIRST PENETRATIONS
MLR JAN. 8–23
MABATANG
ABUCAY
PILAR
MAUBAN
I CORPS
II CORPS
ORION
MLR JAN. 26–APR. 7
LIMAY
Manila Bay
CABCABEN
BATTLE OF THE POINTS
LA MONJA
CORREGIDOR
CABALLO
EL FRAILE
CARABAO
TERNATE
Situation on Bataan
January–April, 1942

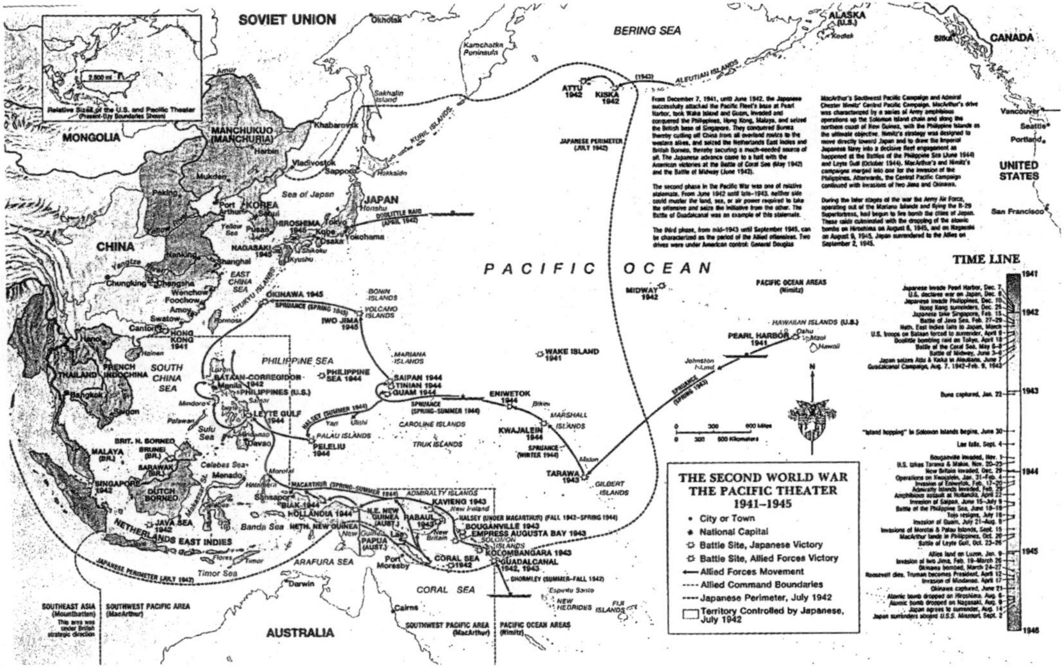

World War II – The Pacific Theater

Map courtesy of the West Point Museum Collections, United States Military Academy

The Men of Triumphs and Tragedies

Actual Names Used:

General Douglas MacArthur
Lieutenant General Jonathan Wainwright
First Sergeant Brady
Colonel Chase
Dr. Overton
Japanese General Homma Masaharu
Japanese Emperor Hirohito
Japanese Warlord Hideki Tojo

Actual Men Given Fictitious Names:

Corregidor

Captain I.M. Wacko
Chaplain Ive Gottit
Lieutenant Snooze

Members of the Special Duty Squad

Colonel Can Do
Red
Casey
Parks
Joe
Hard Nose

POW Camps, Japan

Aomi

Kirby
O'Brien
Rabbit Ass
Preacher
Doctor Do Good
Doctor Cut Up
Johnnie

Tanagawa

Hangnecker (interpreter)
Dale

The Flight of the Ore Car
March–June 1945

ON A SPRING DAY IN 1945, SIX HUNDRED BREATHING skeletons marched back up through the wildflowers gracing a mountainside of northern Japan. We counted off, then found our work partners and tram cars. We POW slaves repeated what had become insanity, loading ore from Mitsui's mine at Camp Aomi as we slowly starved to death. We had done the same thing every day for years, hour after hour, day after day, month after month, in hot and cold weather—always starving, but for me, never hopeless.

Plenty of the men I'd known since becoming a POW had lost hope that we'd ever be rescued or see the States again. They'd given up and eventually died. I had hope. A Japanese doctor in the first prison camp I was sent to caused it. After my encounter with him, I refused to give up. I set my teeth against it.

My partner, Kirby, and I had talked a few times about shoving our car off in the crusher and shutting the whole operation down. We'd made sure no one was around to hear us—POW or supervisor. Some of them would sell you out for an extra bowl of rice. Maybe Kirby and I meant to do it. Maybe we'd plotted to pass time. I don't know, but we knew none of us could go on doing what the Japanese required and stay alive.

That morning, we grabbed the first car out. We pushed all the way to the far end of the loading area of the mine. Kirby started shoveling. "We gonna do it? Today?" he half-said, half-asked.

I could tell he was looking at me. Dangerous.

I dug away, just like always. Finally, I looked up at him. His eyes were round as half-dollars. I wasn't sure if the skull his face had become made them look like that, or whether it was the fear that came with his determination to take control of our lives. I wondered what my eyes looked like. Finally, I whispered, "It's possible they'll kill us for it, Kirby." To keep the supervisors from becoming suspicious, I looked back down at the rock and dirt we dug, and added, "What's the difference? We die shutting her down so at least the other guys have a chance, or die working ourselves to death. I say, let's go for it."

He nodded.

We finished filling the tram car, threw down our tools, and Kirby said, "This is it, Bake. If you want to change your mind, better say so now." I think he'd meant to grin then, but he grimaced instead.

"Let's do 'er," I answered.

We waited for all the others to clear the main track so we had a straight shot down to the crusher.

On Kirby's "Go!" we released the brakes on our tram car, jumped on the rear platform and took our last ride down to the scale. We didn't hold the car back like on a normal run, so it gained more and more speed down the long grade toward the scale. The wind was blowing what little hair I had left. The mountainside flashed by. The sky was spring blue. I think I even heard a bird sing. Kirby started screaming like a banshee. The faces of amazed Japanese guards, supervisors and POWs alike streaked past. It must have been a mile down to the crusher. "Goodbye, scale!" I yelled as we neared, and joined Kirby in his hollering. We leaped from the car just before it sped into the crusher with no steel bar on the back.

That tram car, ore and all, catapulted into the crusher. Rocks crashed. Metal screamed as gears were roughed up. Belts flew off. The whole thing shut down in a matter of moments. The wheels of industry were suddenly halted. I wanted so much to laugh and give old Kirby the high five, but we needed to act as if something had gone wrong. So I stood there looking as bewildered as I could muster.

The Japanese supervisors and guards went mad! I had not seen so many furious Japanese in one place at one time since Monkey Point on Corregidor in the Philippine Islands. There was no doubt who was responsible for running the car into the crusher, and we hadn't fooled them with our acting. They came at us with blood in their eyes.

I found myself on the ground, rolled into a human knot, mindlessly trying to protect my face and head as I writhed among the kicks and stomps of those Japanese workboots. They kicked my back so hard I couldn't hang onto my knees, and when I came unrolled, they'd go for my stomach and head. I rolled myself back into a knot again and again, refusing to let them make me yell. I thought I could feel my bones breaking. They battered and bruised me, and still they stomped my back. Their fury could not be satisfied. They gave me the worst beating I ever experienced.

Under their screaming, I heard Kirby groaning, and maybe that woke me up. Nothing before in my POW experience equaled this, and certainly not in my civilian life. I expect the same was true for Kirby. I began to think they'd never stop, and sent up a fast prayer—"Lord, You've brought us this far! Please keep them from killing us now." I was grateful that what I call my hope transplant—something that happened at Tanagawa, the first Japanese POW camp I lived in—was in place and working well. The hope transplant and the prayer, once again, saved my life. At least, after a few more kicks, the boots stopped thudding into our bodies.

The Japanese decided to hold a kangaroo court. Though it was 1945 and we'd been POWs several years, the Japanese still communicated with us mostly through gestures and yelled words we frequently didn't understand. They first sentenced Kirby, who was not in any better shape than I was, and me to the task of removing the tram car from the crusher. We were let down on ropes with instructions to remove the car. I felt wobbly, like one of those marionettes on strings. We had no opportunity to talk because the guards hovered above us, and we looked at the rubble of our handiwork knowing full well there wasn't a prayer we, or anyone, would get that car out of the crusher.

I found out later it was not a bad afternoon for the rest of that work detail, because no one could work. All cars were soon loaded and in line to be dumped, but all anyone could do was stand around, look on, and wait. It soon became a standoff of the first degree. We could not have gotten that car out of there if we had wanted to. The mine was permanently shut down. Nevertheless, we were in the crusher all afternoon, acting like we were heaving and tugging on any part that we could reach. Our inability to do the impossible did give us a little time to rest our trampled, bloody bodies. All those Japanese supervisors and guards waited, along with the whole POW detail, and the POWs needed the rest.

The reprieve did not last past afternoon, however. Someone came to the conclusion that their sentence was not working out as planned. Kirby and I were lifted out of the crusher amid a few more well-aimed kicks. Then three of the Japanese supervisors tried their hands at removing the tram car. They had about as much luck as we did. Finally, the whole crew returned to camp, as many POWs as could get away with it giving Kirby and me thumbs-up.

Stumbling back to camp, I asked Kirby, "Do you believe in fortune tellers?"

He just shrugged his shoulders.

I continued, trying to bring back our positive attitude, "In September of '40 at the Tri-State Fair in Amarillo, Texas, one told me, 'You will soon be going on a very long trip.'"

Kirby half-grinned, keeping his head down.

"If she'd mentioned some of these potholes," I added, "I may not have come."

His grin widened. Ol' Kirby would make it.

That started me thinking about all that had happened since that fair.

Country Boy Studies War
November 1940–January 1941

THAT LONG TRIP HAD BEGUN FOR ME ON THE DAY I ANSWERED the call of the United States for young men to strengthen our Army. It was January 1941. I'd hitched a ride into Amarillo, Texas.

Shivering a little, I looked in the passenger side rearview mirror of the *Amarillo Daily News* truck. The hint of light in the eastern sky over my hometown of McLean, Texas, promised morning. I headed west and McLean disappeared behind me down Route 66.

Hank, the bulk newspaper carrier, said, "Well, son, I served in the Big One back in the teens. I s'pose this one could get as big as that one. We never thought it would, but now I don't know."

Turning to look at the white hair on the side of his head, I observed, "Everybody in McLean thinks we'll end up in it." I wouldn't say I knew Hank real well, but well enough to hitch a ride.

"Can't see how we can keep from it. I think that's why

you're headed wherever you're headed."

Hank, like most folks in west Texas, wasn't one to talk a lot. We came from pioneer stock who braved the elements to eke out a living—people who considered talking a luxury not to be wasted. Hank fell silent, and my thoughts began to wander back over the last few months.

Germany had occupied most of Europe. England held out only because of the American supply line and the courage of her people. Japan had ravaged Korea and China. She was buying all the scrap metal and other supplies she could get from the US. This gave the country folks from the Dust Bowl a chance to make a little money on their old plows and farm equipment, effectively ending the Depression. Men were taking home a paycheck again. The US sold some old freighter-type ships for scrap that Japan would later use against our troops. President Roosevelt had recently been elected to his third term in office. His Fireside Chats came over radio, which was brand new at the time, giving my family a larger view of events happening in the world. Two months ago, in November of 1940, Congress had passed the first military draft. So it hadn't taken a lot of brains, even for country boys like me, to know we were headed for war.

Roosevelt said, "If you attack the US, you better carry a big stick." England said, "We will never surrender." Japan said, "Asia for the Asians." And so the rhetoric went. Every man eighteen to forty years of age had to register for the draft. I registered, and so did my brothers, G.F. and Irvin. We all agreed we wanted to defend our country when it became necessary. Our Armed Forces numbered very low. They had to be built up, and we stood up to fortify them.

The morning of registration had brought a long line of men. I got off the night shift at the Ford Texaco dealership, ate breakfast, and registered before going home. My draft number was 501, so I would go in the second batch of 500, before G.F. and Irvin. I desired no excuse. I was twenty-two, healthy, working, and America needed young men. I was the second man from McLean, Texas, to leave in early January 1941.

The day before, I'd said goodbye to my family. After finishing the night shift I had felt tired, but I enjoyed a few moments talking to Mom's tiny back as she quickly shifted right, then left, then right again, washing up the breakfast dishes. My parents worked hard, Mom at home and Dad at the cotton gin. Dad had raised my brothers, sisters, and me to work hard, too, on our cotton farm. That is, until the Depression took it from us. Now, Dad worked at the gin most of the time. He was there now. I loved my dad. He'd brought us through hard times in the Depression with his positive attitude about life. I'd heard him say a thousand times, "Times may be hard, they often are. However, when you are up against a stump, you can sit on it or keep pushing." I have always chosen the latter—that's what my dad expected.

"You make sure to keep your feet clean and wear heavy socks," Mom said, without turning from her work. "I've heard they just march you all over, and if you get blisters on your feet, that's going to be mighty hard on you."

The war news from the "newfangled" radio I'd bought Mom and Dad for Christmas joined the sound of icicles cracking off the roof as the sun rose higher in the Texas Panhandle sky. It competed with Mom's voice. Nevertheless, I responded to her.

"Mom, I'll take care of myself, just the way you taught us," I replied.

She dried her hands on a flour-sack towel. "Good. Well, then. It's wash day—be sure to put your laundry in the hamper."

"Yes ma'am."

Monday. My mother had washed our laundry using the ribbed washboard on Mondays for as long as I could remember. This would be the last time she did mine for a while. We didn't say anything about my leaving. I'd already told her I wanted to serve my country. She'd already told me she felt proud of me and would pray for me every day I was gone. Today, few words passed between us. Since they couldn't express everything we already knew we felt about each other and the war, more words might even do it an injustice.

The news ended and the radio announcer said, "This is Station KGNC, Amarillo, Texas. It is 7:52 a.m."

"Well, I better get some sleep," I said. I didn't need a lot of sleep after night shifts, but at least a few hours.

"Of course," she replied, and turned to look at me. She came across the kitchen then. I stood to meet her and she hugged my waist. She'd made every one of her children attend Sunday school every Sunday of our lives, all my eight brothers and sisters. I knew she really would wait at home praying for every one of her boys while we fought the coming war.

When the first man from our county—Hugg was his name—had left in December, the townspeople of McLean turned out in force to cheer him on. For me, my friends, our parents, the whole town, this war was about freedom. Our country's founded on freedom, and we stood ready to do anything required to defend that freedom, whether we were the men who'd fight or the people who'd stay at home supporting us. My leaving would be different than Hugg's—I would be gone before first light. There would be no crowds.

After a four-hour nap, I drove my '31 Model A down McLean's main street, through our one stop light, over to say goodbye to my best friends, Johnnie Mertel and Dewey Hood. Johnnie worked at his dad's dry goods store. He asked his Dad for an hour or two off and we walked over to Dewey's cafe.

Wiping the counter, Dewey asked, "How you gettin' to Amarillo tomorrow?"

I handed him a nickel for a cup of coffee. "Goin' up with Hank," I said.

He waved off my money.

Pouring the coffee, Dewey asked, "Art, you think Roosevelt and Churchill can win this war?"

Johnnie drummed his fingers on the counter. "That business about the big stick sounds pretty serious to me. Only our army isn't very big." He stood and put one foot on his stool, saluting me. "Put me in there, put you guys and all the others in there, we're young and tough just like America, and we'll win it." He broke the salute. I figured the next thing we knew, he'd be singing *The Star Spangled Banner*.

"Appears to me we've got to win it. I sure don't want to be working for Hitler, or Tojo either," I said.

Dewey handed me my cup of coffee. "I'll keep your A tuned for you 'til they call me. You want me to drive 'er? I'd make sure she idles slow down Main," he offered, a little tongue-in-cheek about the idle.

"Naw, Dewey, I've got 'er sold." The coffee tasted hot and bitter, just the way I liked it.

"Oh, well, I think I'm going to enlist anyhow," he said, taking another swipe at the counter. He glanced sideways at me with a silly grin and added, "I'd just as soon go with you as with a bunch of strangers."

"That would be real good," I said. I'd hardly been out of Texas, and having someone I knew go with me would be better than good, especially since it was going to be Dewey. We discussed the war for an hour or two, and then I set my coffee cup down. "Well, I'm goin' out to say goodbye to Louise."

Louise cried and promised to wait for me until the river dried up. She'd always been given to exaggeration. I told her not to worry, I'd be back when we'd won the war, and we'd take up right where we'd left off. After I'd told her goodbye, I drove back through town on the way home. As I drove by the florist, I wondered how Mom would get my flowers and candy on Mother's Day, and thought I'd wire money from wherever I landed.

When I got home, Dad had come in from the gin, and my brother and sister, G.F. and Susie, from school. We had my favorite dinner—pork chops, mashed potatoes and country gravy—and hugged each other good night and goodbye, since they wouldn't be up in the morning when I left.

Now, I took a mental picture of the rolling grass of the high plains of Texas that stretched to the horizon as the newspaper truck rolled down 66. I loved this country where my family had set its roots. I even loved the unpredictable ice and dust storms, the power of the tornadoes. This was home.

Hank dropped me off at the post office in Amarillo around five. Some other men and I went down to the basement, where we were told to fill out papers and strip down to our skivvies for the medical examination. The doctor came in about eight a.m., looked over at us, and said, "What are you guys doing, standing over there naked? Don't you know you're in the Army now?"

The Army had signed up twenty of us by nine that morning, put us aboard a train to the Lubbock, Texas, Regional Induction Center, and from there a troop train to California.

Assess Your Options and Use What You Have

January–November 1941

WE "SOLDIER BOYS," AS WE WERE POPULARLY CALLED, arrived in San Francisco three days later. By ferry we sailed to Fort McDowell, on Angel Island in San Francisco Bay—a hilly island east of the Golden Gate Bridge and the Marin headlands. I positioned myself in the bow of the ferry, the salt spray drenching me thoroughly, because I wanted to get the feel of the ocean.

I'd not seen ocean in McLean, and never sailed upon it. The salt wind blew my hair back and clouded my vision, but not enough to miss the expanse of this blue-black water. Even though this was only the bay, it went on nearly forever, like the plains of grass at home.

Angel Island sits at the mouth of the Sacramento River, where its fresh water dumps silt into the salt water of San Francisco Bay. Eucalyptus trees planted by the military greeted us at the entrance to Fort McDowell. McDowell's north barracks, where I was posted, had served as the immigration station for the Chinese during the building of the transcontinental railroad. Its triple-deck, five-foot long bunks were sure "comfortable" for a six-foot country boy like me! However, back when the Chinese were interned there, the whalers had burned every tree on the island for firewood. Since then, the Army had replanted with exotic varieties of trees and other plants not native to the area. So, it may not have been too comfortable at night, but it was a pretty place to begin a stint in the service.

The officers gave us an IQ test, a lesson about Army life, and three choices for boot camp: El Paso, Texas; Alaska; or the Philippines. Since I didn't want the desert heat of El Paso or the cold of Alaska, I chose the Philippines.

My choice bought me two more months in San Francisco, because the government couldn't send a draftee overseas. I was discharged and then reenlisted as a volunteer. The time it took to get this paperwork through afforded me and the other new soldiers the chance to see San Francisco. It also gave Dewey a chance to catch up with me.

I was checking the shine on my shoes one morning, getting ready to head over to the mess hall, when I heard, "Hey, Bake, that you?"

I knew that voice before I even turned around. "Dewey!" I yelled. "How about that, man, you *did* catch up with me."

Grinning, he clapped me on the back. "Always stand by my word," he said. "You been over to San Francisco yet?"

"Once, we rode cable cars, saw Fisherman's Wharf. What a place!"

"I heard until they ship us out we've got twenty-one big ones a month to enjoy ourselves with," he said.

"Yep. I can't find anybody who'll take my money, though. Soon as they see the uniform, they wave it off."

We hitched the ferry, then strolled up and down Broadway, our heads up and mouths hanging open at those skyscrapers. That afternoon, we hollered our heads off riding the breathtaking roller coaster at Ocean Beach several times, and every chance we got after that. Nothing ever sent my stomach to my mouth like that in Texas. Twenty-one dollars never has added up to much in San Francisco, so we didn't try any of the ritzy places, but we had a good time.

One day when we arrived back on Angel Island, the sergeant in charge said, "You guys get your duffle bags loaded—you're out of here in the morning."

Dewey glanced at me and I smiled. We were finally on our way, and we were glad. Though we'd had fun, we hadn't joined up to ride roller coasters.

"Sarg, where we goin'?" Dewey asked.

The sergeant had already walked down to the end of the barracks and was about to go out the door. He yelled over his shoulder, "You asked for the Philippines. Looks like you got it."

Dewey and I steamed under the Golden Gate Bridge on the troop ship *Republic* on March 31, 1941. After we got past the swells just outside the Golden Gate, it was a smooth ride. The Pacific Ocean is a wonder. More water in one place than a Texas boy ever imagined, as far as you could see, clear to where the horizon met the sky, all the way around you. The *Republic* was gunmetal gray with metal floors, metal walls, metal stairs. Dewey and I spent our time playing pinochle, writing a letter home now and then, and speculating about what we were headed for.

An old master sergeant sailed on the *Republic* with us. He'd been to the Philippines before, and was headed back to help whip all the young recruits into shape.

One day, this master sergeant gathered some of us and gave us a little rundown on our destination. He unfolded a map on the deck, squatted down in front of it, and pointed to an island in the mouth of Manila Harbor. "Corregidor, which we more often refer to as 'The Rock,'" he said, "is an 1800-acre island shaped like a polliwog swimming out in the mouth of Manila Bay."

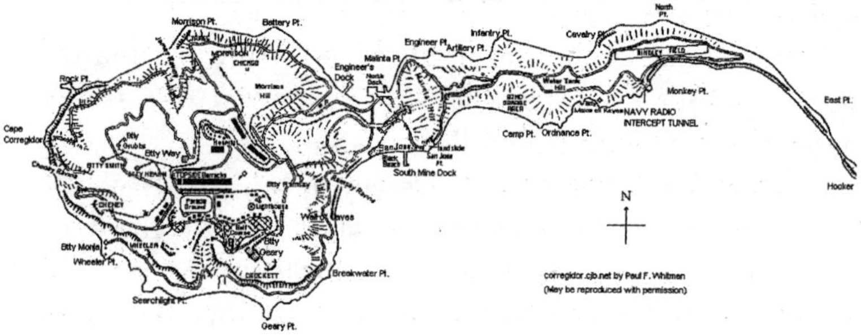

corregidor.cjb.net by Paul F. Whitman
(May be reproduced with permission)

"The largest portion of the island is all mountain. It is broken into what we call Top Side, Middle Side, and finally Bottom Side, where the docks are. Then a small mountain rises toward the tail of the island. It's called Malinta Hill. The tail is called Monkey Point." There was some laughter at that. He looked up for silence, shifted his weight onto his other foot, and continued.

"After WWI, we heavily fortified Corregidor with large naval guns pointed toward the China Sea. There are also eight-inch mortars. Then there is a battalion of three-inch mobile anti-aircraft (AA) guns, searchlights and guidance systems (the 60th Coast Artillery AA), plus some five-inch guns and fifty-caliber machine guns for support."

Pointing to indicate areas he was talking about, he said, "Top Side has barracks, the post exchange, officers' housing, a theater, parade grounds, and support buildings, but you won't be seeing any of them until later because you'll be at the mile-long barracks at Middle Side. Boot camp personnel are housed there with the military police (MPs) and the guardhouse. Off to the side of that is the base hospital.

"Around the Bottom Side docks are warehouses and support structure, as well as a small Filipino village where many of the civilian workers live."

A soldier in the back of the group asked, "Filipina girls pretty?"

"Barrio is off limits," the sergeant responded without looking up, and continued, "Between Bottom Side and Monkey Point, and through Malinta Hill, is a tunnel with a two-way highway running through it. It is constantly guarded by MPs because there are lateral tunnels sprouting off from the main one where emergency food and ammo are stored. The tunnel also contains an emergency general command post, plus a hospital."

This sergeant wasn't any spring chicken, and I was beginning to wonder how long his knees would hold out squatting like that. However, he just kept right on talking and pointing out places on the map.

"Monkey Point is a long ridge that forms the 'tail' of the polliwog. It has a long beach on the north, and there is a rocky shore on the south. The beach on the north is the only useable beach on Corregidor. Our main forces are in

Manila, but you all are going to Corregidor to defend Manila if the need arises." He folded up the map and got to his feet, not showing a single sign of stiffness. That completed our training during the boat ride over.

We landed in Manila Harbor on April 22, and were ferried to Corregidor. After we settled into Middle Side, we had an evening meal.

"Man, Dewey, this limeade tastes darn good," I said, pouring myself a third glass. "I prefer the milk," he said. "I just love milk. I'm pretty fond of being on dry land, too," he said, patting the bench next to him for emphasis. Dewey had had a little problem with seasickness on the way over.

I had finished up dinner and was getting up to march out of the mess hall, when I got sick as a horse. I bent over, heaved, and then ran for the latrine. I would have gladly taken to my bed, but we had to march over to the theater and watch *Gone With the Wind*, all four hours of it, instead. I don't know what was wrong with that limeade, but I steered clear of the stuff from that day on. Man, I was ready for bed that night!

The next morning we met Colonel Chase, our commander. At first light, we lined up on the parade ground outside the barracks for his review. A small man in stature, who had served in the US Army since the horse cavalry days, he stood straight as a ramrod. "Men," he said, "I am hard as nails. *You* will become hard as nails during this boot camp. That is your goal." He returned the salute of the lieutenant in charge, strode to his Jeep, and was gone.

Boot camp was made up of city kids and country kids, many from Texas and New York, eighteen to twenty-two years old, learning to become fighting men in the tropical heat of the South Pacific. We were quarantined and fed good regular meals, but the days grew long with learning to march and doing calisthenics to take off fatty tissue and replace it with muscle. It was hot, and it was all work—a world away from family and home.

One morning we hit the deck before dawn, as usual, dressed in our tropics uniforms, gobbled some grub in the mess hall, and upon emerging found a pile of 30-06 Springfield bolt-action rifles awaiting us. Each man took a rifle and five rounds of live ammo. We took the rifle apart, cleaned it, reassembled it, and got ready for the firing range that afternoon.

Dewey said, "Now, this is more like it. How you gonna have a war with no weapon?"

I sat polishing the black metal. This wasn't new to me, didn't seem like more war or less war. Every man in Texas had a rifle—rifles didn't make a war. We finished up the cleaning about noon and went into our barracks. I kicked my boots off and laid down on my bunk for a little rest.

About that time, one of the rifles fired down at the other end of the barracks. It was such a surprise that we all jumped up and ran down there. A soldier lay on the floor, his head a mangled mess. This man had placed his rifle across the gun rack, knelt down with his head to the barrel, pulled the trigger and blown the top of his head off. Maybe rifles did make war real, at least for some soldiers.

"Who is this guy?" I asked.

"Was," Dewey added.

"Just a guy," one soldier said.

"I'll get the lieutenant," another one said. The soldier's death was the first death we'd seen, and not a man of us was left unsombered.

That afternoon we marched to the rifle range. I knew how to use a rifle, and a bull's eye was no problem. I sighted down the barrel, shot, and the bull's eye gave me a little respect from the officers.

The next day we were issued our full field packs, rifle, and ammo belt with ammo, in preparation for our road march. That march completed boot camp. We marched from the parade ground to place of duty. It was nine miles around that mountain. You completed it one mile regular time and one mile double-time, but you made it—or you did the whole boot camp over again. Maybe more important, you did it or you weren't ready for war conditions.

When we got to the Top Side parade ground, Col. Chase performed a full field inspection. Those who passed inspection were sent to duty. If not, they went back to boot camp for another try. Dewey and I set up our half pup tent, displayed all our gear for inspection, and then stood at attention while Col. Chase inspected our equipment and rifles. We passed!

I was assigned to Headquarters Battery of the 60th Coast Artillery AA, barracked on Top Side. Dewey went somewhere else and we were separated. I only saw him now and then, and then not at all once the war began.

Our forces in the Philippines had a summer of build up of both men and equipment. I took my Philippine driver's license test and went into truck driving, but that turned out to be hard work. We hauled sandbags, supplies, and/or men all day. Then we dragged those guns around at night on maneuvers. However, it wasn't all bad. We received a shipment of GMC 6x6 trucks with snorkels. Their engines could actually run under water, so you could cross rivers with them.

One Saturday I was driving one, hauling sandbags from the beach. The sergeant in charge of that detail stood watching. "Baker, I wonder if these snorkel trucks really work," he mused. He must have felt like living dangerously that day.

"I sure hope so, or there are going to be some wet soldiers around here," I answered.

"I bet they won't work," he said, looking for a little fun.

"Well, you get these guys to fill this one up with loose sand so I'll have some traction, and I'll just bet it will," I answered, always game for a little mischief.

He had his men load the back of the truck and then yelled, "Check 'er out, private."

I threw it in gear, and the truck started off down the beach to the water. About then I was starting to hope that snorkel really *did* work.

The waves lapped the fenders, and so far, so good. I drove right on, and pretty soon the water had covered the engine. She still chugged right along. Turning horizontal to the island, I waved out the window at the sergeant. I drove her about twenty feet more and then turned to head for dry sand.

Between my waving at the beach and turning to head for it, the transportation officer—our boss—had joined the sergeant. The transportation officer did not look happy. When I drove up next to him and opened the door, the water spotted the bottoms of his khakis. I jumped out, saluted, and said, "Good afternoon, sir."

The transportation officer did not say a word, but he swelled up to about twice the size a human should be. His assistant suggested I return to the barracks.

Needless to say, I lost my Philippine driver's license and my job.

However, lucky for me, there was always some type of duty available on the bulletin board. I got to choose my next assignment. That day, there was a call out for volunteers for a new type of job called "Class 'A' Special Duty." I took the challenge. First, I had to go through boot camp all over again—only this one was much harder.

Special Duty boot camp taught us to travel light and fast in the jungle. We trained to make reconnaissance trips into enemy territory to get needed information. We learned to crawl across the parade ground on our bellies as tracer bullets from machine guns were fired over our heads. We discovered how to search out a good jungle place, where we set up four three-inch guns and oriented them, along with two searchlights and the guidance equipment. We had to get it right, because they all must shoot at the same place ten to twelve thousand feet in the air.

The most important thing we learned, though—one that we used time and again—was *assess your options and use what you have*. The point of this idea was to avoid wasting time whining over what we didn't have and use what we did. The only way to do that was to evaluate what we had available to us or check our possibilities, and use the best one. Assessing your options and using what you had was a strategy that stuck—easy to remember, and easy to apply.

The other guys who wound up in my unit and went through all this training with me were Joe, Casey, Hard Nose, Parks, and Red. Red was my partner, and I could tell he was a man I could trust in a crunch.

Duty in the Philippines was good that summer. We continued the build-up of men and equipment, training, and drilling, of course; but at the same time, I grew to love those tropics. Our Top Side barracks stood wide, with lots of windows looking out on Manila Bay to the east and the China Sea to the west. We enjoyed an ample balcony on both sides, and I saw many a magnificent tropical sunrise and sunset from those balconies. I had gotten a raise, to thirty dollars a month, and the Philippine peso was two for one of our dollars. That gave me sixty pesos to spend each month. Back in Texas, we'd say I was "in high cotton."

For only two pesos, we could hire Philippine civilian workers to do all our barracks work for an entire month. They'd clean, make bunks, shine shoes, do laundry—whatever we needed done. We also hired them to do our kitchen work. The Army furnished two Pale Pilson Philippine beers per day. Times were good.

In August, I experienced my first tropical storm. Winds raged and the rain dropped in sheets, as hard and constant as back in the Panhandle. All those nice windows we'd had in the barracks were blown out, and everything inside got soaked—beds, clothes, gear, *everything*. At the same time, Headquarters had called most of us out to guard officers' quarters or search for three federal prisoners who'd escaped on the island. I was assigned to walk around a general's home on Top Side for two hours on and four hours off, three days and nights. What I remember feeling those days was soggy through and through.

Sometime in August, I received a "Dear John" from Louise. Our mail held too many "goodbye" letters from girls whom soldiers had left at home. The girls all said something along the lines of they couldn't wait for the soldiers anymore and had found fellows who were still at home. Someone named them Dear John letters. We even made up a little ditty that went with them—"Dear John, I brought your saddle home, and hung it on a nail in the barn." Anyway, Louise had found somebody else. I felt disappointed in her. I'd thought she had more character than that.

In September we received a shipload of ROTC officers, lieutenants mostly, from the States. We called these officers "shavetails," because they knew very little about active duty. They were sent to boot camp and they did it all, except the road march and full field inspection. However, much more was expected of them than of the enlisted men. They were to be leaders, officers, and they were not taught to lead during war. I mention this because their lack of knowledge cost at least one of them his life, and, I suspect, the lives of other enlisted men fell to their inexperience.

In October and November, nothing happened other than maneuver practice, mostly at night. We continued to receive men, supplies, and equipment from the States. These were mostly National Guard men and equipment. For the most part they went to Bataan, a thirty-mile-long peninsula that ended north of Corregidor across the narrow stretch of the North Channel.

At about this time, the Philippine Army was integrated into the US Army; we all became known as the US Armed Forces of the Far East (USAFFE). I got a chance to work a little with some of those Philippine Army soldiers, but not much.

Our Class 'A' Special Duty team was split into four units—one major or lieutenant colonel in charge of the team, and one corporal or buck sergeant and five privates per unit. We were on twenty-four-hour call to go and do whatever was needed. Col. Can Do led my unit: Red, Joe, Casey, Hard Nose, Parks, and me.

Then came November 30, 1941. That evening, a lot of the Philippine Armed Forces were on a night maneuver. I was left in the office on Charge of Quarters, which meant to answer the phone and pass along any messages.

Because I was in the office, I heard word come in that the Japanese fleet was at sea and prepared to strike. I remember the tingle on the back of my neck when I realized the preparations we had been making for war were about to be tested. The commander in charge barked into the field phone, "All troops go directly to field positions." The kitchen staff clanged around packing their field kitchen, food, etc., and hurried into the field to serve breakfast, leaving the supply sergeant and me the only ones to occupy our barracks.

War on Corregidor
December 1941–February 1942

WE WAITED. JAPAN WOULD STRIKE SOMEPLACE, AND SOON. There we stood, as a portion of America's front line of defense in the Pacific—Alaska in the north, Hawaiian Islands, Midway, Wake, Guam, and the Philippines. No one knew who would be hit first.

Then Monday morning—December 8 on our side of the International Dateline—my Special Duty squad went on a communication exercise to test equipment. I was positioned on Corregidor, while the others went to an airfield south of Manila named Nichols Field.

As I waited to get their first communication, word came over the radio that Pearl Harbor was under attack by the Japanese. It was Sunday, December 7, 1941, their time, because Pearl Harbor was on the other side of the International Date Line from the Philippines.

None of us knew what else to do, so eventually we calmed down and resumed our wait. But we didn't have long to watch the skies. The Japanese bombed Clark Field in northern Luzon that afternoon. They also made a pass at Nichols Field while our squad was there, but none of us were wounded and all returned safely to Corregidor.

General MacArthur had ordered the thirty B-17 bombers at Clark Field loaded and ready to fly that morning. He had asked Washington for permission to bomb southern Japan that day, but word never came through to give him the OK. So, the Japanese destroyed nineteen of our bombers on the ground that afternoon. Only eleven flew south to Australia that night. Someone said that the general actually cried. Who could blame him?

No doubt about it, the war was on. On December 9, General MacArthur prepared to move his headquarters from Clark Field into Malinta Tunnel. Those in charge began putting the tunnel in shape for wartime service. My unit went about our normal routines, keeping our eyes on the sky.

Finally, since our Special Duty squad had no assignment yet, we put on our helmets and hustled to our new assignment, at Battery "D" of the 60th Coast Artillery AA on Monkey Point. We arrived on December 10, along with the Japanese, who made the first bombing raid on Corregidor that day. The few men left in the barracks came running out in a frenzy. Soldiers yelled, grabbed up rifles, and shot at the sky.

Although the Japanese flew completely out of range of their rifles as well as our three-inch AA guns, everyone went nuts finally having someone to shoot at and fired everything they could. Some even stood in the street, firing handguns at the bombers. I didn't, because it was obvious they were too far out of range, and I was already in the gun pit; but I sure understood the other guys. Lucky for us, the aim of the Japanese was about as bad as ours at that time. All their bombs landed in the China Sea.

However, all of my squad was still on twenty-four-hour call for special duty. Col. Can Do remained stationed with the Headquarters officers, of course. The other six were stationed among gun emplacements on Monkey Point. Red—so named for his curly red hair—was with me at Gun #1, Joe and Parks were together, and Hard Nose and Casey were, too, but I don't recall to which guns they were assigned. Now Red and I had time to get to know each other between bombing raids. We hit it off right away. We both wore our WWI-style helmets at a jaunty angle, so to speak. Red was a long, tall fellow from Brooklyn—a real likable guy. We both had a little rascal in us, so we enjoyed adventures on Corregidor.

Hard Nose and Casey enjoyed being partners, too. They liked to get drunk and fight. Hard Nose had been an oil field worker. He and Casey also enjoyed their honky-tonking.

I'm not sure how Joe and Parks felt about each other. Joe was a good-looking guy who loved motorcycles. That's all I knew about him. Parks had been in the regular army, and over time he had learned to whine pretty often. Col. Can Do became noticeably weary of Parks' whining.

People familiar with World War II in the South Pacific may have heard of the mystery of the opening of Malinta Tunnel. Most who were there had a personal perception that the tunnel held food, from listening to lectures and seeing movies showing how the idea was formed and completed for this tunnel. We saw pictures of row after row of beef halves. We understood there would be at least six months' supply, should anyone try to conquer the

"Rock." We saw pictures of empty office space awaiting a day of emergency. There was a vacant hospital, lit from top to bottom by built-in power generators. We could hold out forever—nothing to worry about. We expected to defend Manila for as long as it took.

However, Japan had decided to come in the "back door" of the Philippines. Instead of facing our guns, pointed at the China Sea at the mouth of Manila Bay, they landed at Lingayen Gulf to the north, because no one blockaded the path of ships in the north China Sea where it was located. Our leaders had concentrated on defending Manila at Manila Bay, at Corregidor. By choosing Lingayen Gulf, the Japanese had caught us unprepared. They had begun their march down the island of Luzon to Manila from there.

Malinta Tunnel was opened to accommodate operating the war on the Philippines from Corregidor. The tunnel housed the offices for General MacArthur and his staff. The emergency hospital was there, like we'd been told, well lighted and ready for use by the doctors, nurses, and patients transferred from the hospital at Middle Side. However, when they opened the refrigerated vault and touched the beef sides, they turned to dust. Why? Tags still on the meat indicated the vault had been filled and sealed in 1917 and 18—during and directly after WWI—so, refrigeration did not keep the meat fresh for twenty-four years. Period.

We now were told we had three months' supply of food. The commanders said if we could hold out until March, a convoy from the States would arrive. It would provide all the food we needed, plus more men and supplies to win our victory. Still no need to worry.

What to do? What common sense solution was there? *Assess your options, and use what you have.* Our obvious answer to the food problem: live with it!

What about the upcoming battle for Monkey Point? That became our primary concern, because Monkey Point was the only place to land on Corregidor, and it was directly across the channel from the Bataan Peninsula. (Some of my dates and times may be off a little—after the war, an Army agent who debriefed me took my notes and datebook as evidence for war crimes trials. I never got them back.)

Battery D's three-inch AA guns, search light, plus guidance system were positioned along the top of that long ridge, Monkey Point. We'd dug in about three feet, positioned these huge guns on caissons, and then used sandbags to form an eight-foot wall of protection. The bombs and shells, then, needed to hit us directly in order to put a gun out of order when they shelled us. If the hit was a little low, it would explode against the hillside. If it went a little high, it went on its way to wherever. We were prepared for the long haul.

There was also a fifty-caliber machine-gun battery on Monkey Point. I do not remember the name. They protected the AA battery from strafing. A few men with bulldozers from the engineers also did work on roads and the airstrip. I don't know why they repaired the airstrip—all planes were out of service—but that road down the north side of the ridge and the other down the south side were important. Those roads provided the only way in or out of Monkey Point.

It wasn't long until the command post on Monkey Point was turned over to First Sergeant Brady, who was a jewel. The sergeant stood about six-foot-four and certainly had the stature to push us all around if he'd wanted to, but he never did. He was a natural commander who quickly earned the respect of all his men.

He set up his command post on top of a water tower among the three-inch guns. If our communication line went out, which it often did, Sgt. Brady used his megaphone, or bullhorn, as he called it. He could yell loud enough to give us orders. A long-time soldier in the US Army, he used to say he went to WWI and did not care whether he came home or not, but in WWII, he wanted to survive. I never saw him out of uniform, and not very often without his helmet.

The Japanese bombed us every day. We all learned to dread the whistle of the falling bomb, the concussion of the explosion, shrapnel and debris flying everywhere. Fear rode our backs. Before long, the Japanese had learned how to aim their bombs and had destroyed every sprout of the vegetation on Monkey Point. We responded to every raid, learning to triangulate our gun, the guidance computer, and the planes. We shot many bombers out of the sky, but soon we fell short of three-inch ammo. At that point, we were ordered to shoot six rationed shots per gun per air raid. We had to aim straight!

Our procedure was to load those three-inch shells, weighing about twenty-eight to thirty pounds apiece. The gun crew could fire twenty-five or thirty rounds per minute. Then we cut fuses, so that the shells would explode at 10,000–12,000 feet in the air. Each high-explosive shell was effective on a plane within a fifty-yard radius. It did not take long, less than ten seconds, to fire six shots per gun.

When the bombers came in, we could hear the roar of

their engines before we saw them. They bombed mostly in the morning, flying in from the east. That way, they took advantage of flying from a position where we had to look right into the sun. This made it impossible to see them until they had flown nearly on top of us. However, when they put their planes on autopilot to make a smooth bomb run, we could compute their height, speed, dirсction, and wind speed with our computerized guidance systems, cut the fuses accordingly, and fire our six shots.

After we finished firing, we'd watch their bombs drop, listening to that whistling descent to the ground. We could even tell about where they would land. The smell of burning gunpowder began to hang in the air over Monkey Point. As I said, we didn't need to run, because it took a direct hit for a bomb to compromise a bunker. If it was going to hit right on your bunker, no amount of running would save you anyway.

At about the same time, we could see our pattern of twenty-four shells bursting in air as the planes, hopefully, flew through the pattern.

One day we were firing away when a shell came in from across the channel, burst close by, and a piece of shrapnel hit the recoil slide of our gun. That gun jammed in a recoiled position with a thud. What a jolt for the gun crew. No one was hurt much, but the gun had to be removed from the pit and sent to ordinance for repair.

"What are we supposed to shoot with now, our fingers?" Red said to no one in particular. He spoke the desperation we all felt. Nobody answered him. I just started unscrewing one of the bolts. Complaining didn't change the fact that our gun was down. Our only option was to get the gun repaired, so we might as well get to it.

The guns had legs extending from each side to balance them. We had to climb over the legs when the guns were set up in the pits. Once we'd folded up the legs and pulled the gun out of the pit with a truck, we got it off to ordinance. We did this and all our outside work at night, because the Japanese were watching and shooting.

When the gun was fixed, they trucked it back, and we got things ready to move it into the pit. However, our captain, whom I've renamed I.M. Wacko—appropriately, I think—showed up.

"Let's take my Jeep, go find some men to come help us, and we'll push it into the pit," he said.

No one said a word. Red gave me a look under the bill of his cap that said, "Is this guy totally *nuts*?" No one moved forward to go with him. There was no way any number of men had the strength to push that huge gun into the pit.

Captain Wacko and his driver finally jumped into his Jeep and took off to look for helpers. While he was gone, we borrowed a bulldozer sitting close by, pushed the gun into the pit with it, and got it set up and oriented—all before the captain got back.

He arrived with no men to help, naturally, but he sure blew his top when he saw that gun in place. "Who did this?" he yelled. "I'll court martial the lot of you!"

We just kept our mouths shut and eventually went to bed.

Another day when the bombers came in during the afternoon, a tug with a barge was chugging along toward the Bottom Side dock. The bombers hit it, and it sank just off our beach. Sgt. Brady sent a detail down to see if we could find some extra food. We hadn't been eating much since the Japanese began bombing us. The barge was loaded with liquor. We had an exceptionally good time that evening.

The next morning our shavetail lieutenant—I'll call him Lt. Snooze—decided we should haul the liquor to shore and report it to Headquarters. He hoped to score a couple of points for himself with the commanders.

We went down to the beach and worked all morning at unloading the barge. He sat nearby, seeing that we put it all on the stack. However, one of us, Casey, I think, had found a five-gallon cask of native rum among the liquor. We set it to one side, acting like it was a case of water, and got drunk as skunks as we worked. That treasure from the sea gave us a little relief during that daily, never-ending bombing of Corregidor.

The surrender of Malinta Tunnel, 1942.

Heroes Fall on Bataan and Corregidor
March–May 1942

THROUGHOUT THE WINTER AND SPRING, WE WERE SHORT OF food. Sgt. Brady constantly searched for ways to supplement our meager rations. One day we noticed a lot of activity on Bottom Side—could a shipment of food have come in? How could we find out? *Assess your options and use what you have,* to the rescue again.

Red and I volunteered to go down and assess the situation. We got up at two a.m., sneaked around the north side of Malinta Hill, and were nosing around the warehouses just after daylight. As I began to pull a door open, I heard the siren sound for a bomb raid.

"They always bomb the Point—let's get up on the roof and see the show," I said.

Red beat me to the ladder. As I followed him over the top of the roof, a Japanese dive-bomber flew right over our heads, followed by several others, dropping bombs all around us. They were right on top of us, so close I felt like they were after me. It seems they knew what was in the warehouse and we did not. It was the only time I was personally involved with dive-bombers.

"Darn those Japs, anyway!" Red yelled. We scrambled for cover.

They had also seen the activity on Bottom Side, and decided to bomb the warehouses. I think they may have known it wasn't food causing the activity. Our forces had desired more room in Malinta Tunnel, so the heavy ammo for the larger naval guns was being moved from there into the warehouses.

When the ammo began to explode, the projectiles were too heavy to be moved, so the shell casings would fly through the air. Man, what a morning! We scrambled out of the way of one shell casing after another. I was out of breath and sweating, whether from fear or running, I'm not sure. Soon we knew what every one of those warehouses held, and we didn't even wind up with any food. As the raid continued, the black smoke got thick, and we dodged those casings whistling out of the blackness most of the morning.

When we finally got out, I looked at Red and said, "You are black as the ace of spades!"

He replied, "Welcome to the club, brother. Let's cut through the tunnel and get back where we belong, while we're still alive to tell it."

At the mouth of the tunnel, the guards said, "Soldiers, what are you doing out during a raid?"

"We were out on water detail and got caught," Red said, at what I considered a pretty fast pace for concocting a lie. The guard in charge looked him over and said, "I guess that's as good a story as any," and allowed us to enter.

Walking through to the other end, along with the beehive of military personnel, I saw those side tunnels that held the refrigerators where our beef had turned to dust. It occurred to me that small things can change the whole course of history. Who would have thought Corregidor's fate in this war would hinge on a few beef sides?

The guard who met us at the other end of the tunnel said, "A bombing raid is on, and you can't go out right now. You might get hurt."

Red looked at me, and I looked at him, and we laughed until we couldn't breathe. We had to stay in that crowded tunnel until after dark. It was late when we got back to our bunker. Sgt. Brady knew where we'd been, of course, but he couldn't have asked for help for us because we should not have been at Bottom Side in the first place. He could see what had happened that morning, so he thought he had lost a couple of men.

We trudged up that hill, cleared security, and under cover of dark climbed his water tower to report. Sgt. Brady hugged both of us. His arms felt like a bear. Tears ran down his face as he exclaimed, "Oh, my god, you two are a sight for sore eyes!" Pushing both of us back a little, he looked us over and asked, "Are you all right?" We both nodded. Then he started to laugh and slap his leg. When he could finally talk, he said, "You look real good in black."

On another afternoon, two large planes came in from the east, flying at a leisurely pace at about 10,000 feet. Our gun crews got the information from guidance, cut the fuses and fired our six shots per gun, then looked up to watch the show. No bombs dropped. The shells began to burst. One hit a wing about where it connected to the body of the plane—a direct hit. Down plummeted the plane, just off our beach. Man, what a sight!

Our detail sailed out to check before the authorities

could get there. It was a planeload of high-ranking Japanese officers on an inspection trip. I guess they got the correct message—they just didn't take it back to Tokyo.

During this time, the Japanese forces did make one big mistake. They forged down the central valley toward Manila, thinking it would be there that the last-ditch stand would be made. This action on their part allowed the American forces to make a relatively orderly retreat into the Bataan Peninsula, thus prolonging their time in battle considerably. That place would become a battleground for the ages. Those guys were heroes indeed.

At that time, there were a lot of offers for soldiers to transfer to infantry and go to the front lines, which meant Bataan. I don't know how many took the transfer, but I was not interested. I stayed busy with Class 'A' Special Duty activities. Our first real mission came the night General MacArthur and his entourage left the Philippines. The US government relieved him of duty and shipped him to Australia so he could lead US forces when they could return in victory. General Wainwright took command of USAFFE.

Our communication system, mostly field telephones, was in serious trouble. Phone lines lying on the ground constantly got cut, and the phones would go out. Col. Can Do came up with the idea that if we could "borrow" cable—maybe some WWII version of a coaxial cable—we could rig a connection as our phone line and solve a big problem.

We "located" our cable on Bottom Side, got our truck and a rigged-up flatbed trailer, and proceeded to load the spool of cable. The spools were huge and heavy, but why scrimp on quantity? It was all the same price. We had to wait for the MacArthur entourage to leave on their special submarine. Then we watched two seaplanes in the south channel take off, followed quickly by Japanese planes. I don't know about those seaplanes, but MacArthur got out safely.

We began our journey over the narrow, crooked road around the north side of Malinta Hill. It was a very slow, blacked-out trip. A few officers had rigged their quarters in a sort of box canyon on the hillside between the road and the North Channel. They had floors, walls, furniture, but no roofs. That gave us a bird's-eye view. As we slowly made our way around the hillside, one trailer wheel ran off the narrow road on a sharp corner. Down through the thick underbrush went that spool of cable. Men heard the noise and began to run. The cable spool zipped through their playhouses, on down the mountain, across the beach and into the North Channel. Our trip had failed, and there was no chance of "borrowing" another spool. Our first endeavor at a special duty assignment was a wash, so to speak, and we still had our communication problem to deal with.

After General MacArthur left, General Wainwright had serious problems. We had no reconnaissance from the air. Those front line forces at the head of Bataan were taking a real beating. Sure, they killed and wounded lots of Japanese, but more, more, and more poured in. General Wainwright needed to know if the Japanese were bringing in another invasion force.

Col. Can Do decided our unit should go up there and find out. We began our plan to go behind enemy lines, all the way to Lingayen Gulf if necessary, to determine the basic plan of the Japanese. Since we could not go by boat up the coast, or by boat across Manila Bay, we went up Bataan Peninsula, through the US forces' lines, through or around enemy lines.

As we traveled, we made friends. We met men of character on that front-line infantry/command. Those soldiers on the line were super heroes—my hat is *still* off to those guys. They bravely faced impossible odds. They had little food, little ammunition, and far less of an army than the Japanese, and yet they fought on. We slipped through the front line at night.

From there on, we broke new ground all the way. Those Japanese gathered in various groups, with very few security guards. We never knew when we would come upon some of them. However, using our boot camp training at silence and stealth, we could go around the groups with little trouble.

Sure enough, when we got to Lingayen Gulf, shipload after shipload of Japanese soldiers climbed up the beach. No doubt about it, there definitely was another invasion force, and they intended to break that front line of defense on Bataan.

Armed with the information General Wainwright needed, we made our way back through the jungle, about sixty or seventy miles; avoided those Japanese group resting places; flashed the password sign as we crossed no man's land, and found ourselves behind our US forces' lines, ready to head for Col. Can Do.

What we saw at the head of Bataan peninsula was beyond belief. Our USAFFE forces had three lines of infantry, with basically only fifty-caliber machine guns across the head of that peninsula. When the Japanese got hopped up on drugs, yelled "Banzai, Banzai, Banzai," and ran at that line, they would push through or die. It did not take long for dead bodies to cover the barbed wire entanglements. Then live Japanese ran over the top, still yelling.

When Line Number One guns got too hot to fire, Line Number Two began shooting while Line Number One men retreated through Line Number Two. Someone told us that sometimes Line Number Three had to begin shooting before the advance stopped.

It is easy to see why those Japanese needed so many men to defeat our small defense force in the Philippines. Those brave Americans fought on and on, in the face of starvation and dwindling ammunition. Someone estimated the Japanese used two million men against about 27,000 Americans.

We made it back to Corregidor and reported to Col. Can Do, but it was getting late in the day, so to speak, as far as the USAFFE holding out in the Philippines was concerned. Food, supplies, ammo, and nerves ran low. We had no C Rations; our cooks were beginning to boil mules and bring them out to us, telling us they were beef. They tasted pretty good.

Regardless, our unit had another Special Duty job to accomplish. The Japanese had begun firing at us on Corregidor from the south side of the bay. It was especially bad for Monkey Point, because we were nearest to them. What to do? Col. Can Do decided we would go by Philippine small boat across the south channel of Manila Bay to the south of Corregidor. We had a lot of cover that way.

The Filipinos took us over right after dark. They were to pick us up at a set time. This plan allowed a certain number of hours for us to travel along the coast to the small town of Niac, where we determined the long gun fired from. Our mission: find the gun, blow the thing up, fire no shot unless necessary, make our way back to the pick-up spot at the appointed time, and return to

Corregidor. If the Japanese caught us, our commanders would disavow any knowledge of our existence.

We prepared our supplies. Parks, our explosives man, carried his explosives. Because of his experience as a career Army man, Parks could have blown up the headquarters of the Japanese generals and they'd never have known he'd been there. The rest of us would take meager rations, but as much firepower as we could carry in case we had to shoot our way out.

The boat trip was uneventful, other than Parks complaining because he was seasick. We picked our way down the coast, with care and without incident. When we arrived in Niac, we saw that the Japanese had knocked out the back wall of the Catholic church of that small town, moved the gun inside, and stuck the long barrel out a small window in front. They could fire at Monkey Point without being spotted.

"There's no one guarding this place that I can see," Red whispered, as he hunkered down behind a rock fence.

"I guess they expect no trouble," I answered.

"We'll take our positions around the perimeter when they bed down," Hard Nose said. "Protect Parks while he goes in to bomb the gun."

Everything went as planned until Parks set the explosive off. Then those Japanese really came alive. We hustled back out of Niac headed for our assembly area, but they came after our behinds, so we had to shoot our way out.

"They're right on our butts!" Parks yelled. It was becoming easier to pick out landmarks as the sun approached the horizon. We couldn't fire as we ran, and they pounded us all the way to our landing point. Parks had taken the lead. I could hear him yell, "The boat isn't here!"

We hid in the rocks, holding off the Japanese until finally the Filipinos arrived. I was surprised they landed in the hail of bullets, but real glad they did. Scrambling in, I could hear the bullets hitting the water all around us, popping like rocks thrown into a pond.

When we landed on Corregidor, Red said, "I sure am happy to get my feet back on this old rock!"

It was well into the month of March 1942. The only convoy to reach the Philippines was the one that dumped another million Japanese soldiers for those heroes on the front lines of Bataan to contend with. They probably did not have a million bullets left. The empty promise of an American relief convoy was another letdown. Our only option was to sit tight and use what we had on hand, which was precious little. Those air raids continued on Monkey Point, accompanied now by occasional shelling. Our officers still rationed us six rounds per gun per raid.

Lt. Snooze, whom I've mentioned before, was a farm boy from Texas, fresh out of ROTC. He loved his afternoon nap. Corregidor had been a lovely tropical island when we arrived on the Republic, but now only one lonely scrub tree still grew on dusty Monkey Point, about halfway between Gun Pit #1 and Sgt. Brady's command post on the water tower. That is where Lt. Snooze had his personal foxhole dug. We told him a shell or bomb could hit the tree and send shrapnel down on him, but he insisted.

One afternoon during his naptime, the bombers came in from the east as usual. We got our directions and fired our six shots, and then looked up to see what we hit. As we watched those bombs shine in the sunlight coming our way, it became evident that some would come close. The whole gun crew ducked for cover around the edge of our gun pit.

The ground rocked as those bombs hit. Dust flew everywhere. Our gun sergeant arose and asked if anyone was hurt. Our gun crew was all OK, so we began to check others.

We knew Sgt. Brady was OK. He was yelling to others at the top of his voice, trying to find out the condition of all the men. We were all shook up—some needed first aid, but no one in the four gun crews was seriously injured. Only Lt. Snooze didn't respond. When we looked into his foxhole, a sliver of shrapnel about eighteen or twenty inches long lay beside his head. It had come in, hit Lt. Snooze in the neck, and completely cut his head off. At least that young guy did not suffer, but he did pay the price for his lack of training.

Those fresh Japanese troops pressed hard on the front lines of Bataan. With constant shelling and bombs continuing to fall on Corregidor, it did not take a lot of brains to know our time of holdout was nearly over. On April 8, 1942, that front line on Bataan gave way, overwhelmed by an overpowering force of drug-crazed Japanese soldiers. I believe those soldiers were not brave—only drug crazy from narcotics packs I saw each of them carried on his belt.

April 9—Bataan officially surrendered to Japanese General Masaharu Homma. Those brave men had retreated back down the peninsula in front of the Japanese onslaught. Now, General Homma ordered them to march back up that thirty-mile peninsula, plus another thirty-five or forty miles to Camp O'Donnell. Records indicate that of the approximately 11,000 GI's taken, 640 died on that death march, with 1,600 more dying in Camp O'Donnell within six weeks.[1] Soldiers were denied water and killed for as little as falling down. The general paid for this war crime with his life, before a firing squad in

Tokyo, following his trial in 1946.

The Japanese artillery from north of Bataan began moving down the peninsula toward Corregidor. They set up across the North Channel from Monkey Point. The next morning, they took direct aim at our position. They shelled other places on Corregidor, but they had chosen Monkey Point to land on when the time came. They shelled us and bombed us night and day.

Those Japanese knew how to clean up ground where they planned to land. They bombed us—seasoned commanders, privates, shavetail lieutenants, career soldiers, all of us—until nothing stood on Corregidor in the spring of 1942 except on top of a rocky ridge called Monkey Point. On top of that ridge sat a few tough guys who made up 'D' Battery of the 60th Coast Artillery Anti-Aircraft (AA). Only a few months before, we had been known as greenhorn kids from the troop transport ship *Republic*, but today we had our guns in top shape. We hit what we aimed at. Our food and ammo dwindled, with no chance of re-supply, but we fought on.

General Colin Powell was right, during Desert Storm in the 1990s, when he said, "Bombs alone will not bring defeat." The Japanese could have bombed Monkey Point from then on, and if we had had a supply of food, water, and ammo, we would be there still.

That shelling was a completely different ball game. Day and night, those things would hit the side of our hill below us and explode, sending shrapnel everywhere and jarring our eyeteeth. We got no rest whatsoever. Sometimes they would aim high, and the projectile would whistle as it sailed into the south channel. It was a constant, deafening, mind-numbing barrage, day after day.

One Saturday afternoon, Chaplain Ive Gotit came out to minister to the troops. I don't know why he picked that particular Saturday, or why he even came at all—we'd never been graced with his presence before that. He talked to Capt. I.M. Wacko and Sgt. Brady. Sgt. Brady tried to discourage their decision, but to no avail. Capt. Wacko and the chaplain were convinced we needed Communion. They had their crew set up benches between Gun Pit #1 and the water tower. Chaplain Ive Gotit said, "You men need Communion. I'll be back tomorrow morning to officiate."

In the morning we all got out there on those benches. Actually, I don't know if it was all our men or not, but about the time we got started, we heard a *pop-pop-pop*—the sound of artillery fire before the shells arrived. It was no surprise. We'd have been surprised if they *hadn't* fired at us. Everyone ducked back into their gun pits. Chaplain Ive Gotit and crew ducked down to the south shore road home, out of range of the guns, and that was the last we heard of them.

I would be remiss if I did not tell you the truth: there is no Communion in Hell. There was no Communion that day, because war is hell. Have you seen those little red-letter New Testaments the Gideons gave soldiers as they went off to war? I'd been reading the sixteenth chapter of Luke in mine, where Jesus talked with a rich man who had died and gone to Hell. That hell was the real thing. That man was tormented in those flames. He thought just one drop of water would help relieve the torment. Surely he would have appreciated a little cup of grape juice like the chaplain offered us, but Jesus assured him there is no Communion, or peace or water in the real Hell. Let me tell you, Jesus was in my heart on Monkey Point. I had no communion because of the hell of that war, but Jesus never failed me.

Our time on Monkey Point had run out. The Japanese artillery had set up along the south beach of the Bataan Peninsula. They were only three to five miles from Monkey Point. We had no idea where their landing barges would come from, but we knew they would come. We just didn't know when.

Our good Capt. Wacko went completely off his rocker. He blew his top at Sgt. Brady, went back to Malinta Tunnel, and we heard later that he had been relieved of his command. Another captain came out to take over. I don't even remember his name, but the first idea he had was to move down behind the hill, dig a tunnel for protection, then move our three-inch guns down there. We sure couldn't shoot guns from behind a hill, much less a tunnel. He only got a few men to help dig his tunnel, but our guns would stay put. Needless to say, he did not become acquainted with the men of 'D' Battery.

One afternoon, one of the forever falling shells failed to whistle down onto the south shore. It hit Sgt. Brady's water tower. He took the hit. The medics treated him. I heard one say, "The sergeant needs to go to Malinta Tunnel Hospital, but he refuses to leave his post. I'm sure not going to be the one to drag him off that tower."

Sergeant Brady was a soldier indeed. He always gave 110 percent. He was doing it now, and the men trusted him to lead them, even wounded. Another First Sergeant came out who'd been ordered to take his place, but still Sgt. Brady refused to leave. The new man—I never learned his name—was a career soldier also. He was a good man. He knew how to hurry up and wait, and that's the position he took with Sergeant Brady. If Sergeant Brady wanted command, he had it. This new guy never got acquainted with the men of Battery 'D' because he made it his business to kill time rather than rain on Sgt. Brady's parade.

The evening of May 3, Sgt. Brady called a meeting to assess our options. It was sort of lonely on Monkey Point, except for the shelling. There we were, just the gun crews. Our options were to wait it out, or turn tail and run for the tunnel like others had. As always, there was actually only one option—use what we had.

Our inventory of ammo was thirty-six shells. That was nine shells per gun left. We could wait until the Japanese arrived, or shoot at some aircraft. We decided to tear down the north wall of our gun pits that night. Naturally, we would wait as long as possible. When daylight came, the height finder would be opened. The operator would calculate the distance to those Japanese artillery pieces at Cabcabin, with their crews. That information would be fed into the computer and then to our guns, just as if we were shooting at aircraft.

It was decided to burst our high explosive shells about thirty or forty yards in the air over their line of artillery. Our guns would track to the left down the beach as we fired. Our gun crews could fire from twenty-eight to thirty shots per minute under normal circumstances. So our firing time for each gun would be about twenty seconds. Then we could sit back to see what happened before they could return fire. If it did not work and we survived, someone would be court marshaled because it was breaking all the rules, but we were using what we had.

We knew we were there to fight. By this time, we knew that the Japanese were going to take us. The simple truth is that in war, you either kill or are killed. There wasn't time to feel sorry for ourselves or wonder whether we'd get home when we were being shot at constantly. We couldn't think about the Japanese soldiers as men who came to fight for their country just like we did. A person would go crazy doing that. I guess some did. We assessed our options and used what we had. We fought until there was nothing to fight with.

Early in the morning of May 4, our four guns blazed away for about twenty seconds. Then we watched for results, and sure enough, the plan worked—those Japanese were still asleep. It was somehow satisfying, maybe because of Bataan, or Pearl Harbor, or General MacArthur's retreat, to watch their bodies fly through the air, but we had little effect—if any—on their artillery. Those men sure took a beating, though.

However, they recovered rather quickly. Their guns would still fire. They had plenty of men and ammo, so we took a beating like never before. They shelled us for nearly twenty-four hours. All we could do was duck down behind the south wall of our gun pits.

Then, in the early morning of May 5, 1942, their invasion force came across our north beach.

The fifty-caliber machine gun battery plus a few Marines dug in out there were no match at all for their firepower. All we had were small arms, rifles, and pistols. That was no defense at all. They just kept coming and shooting. The beach, and soon Monkey Point, were swarming with Japanese. In front of them, the bodies of Americans carpeted the earth.

Sgt. Brady kept yelling to get down to the south road. That bullhorn was working fine.

Then he got hit. Lost a leg, but he kept yelling orders through the bullhorn.

"No one, and I mean no one, is to try to help me."

Red and I ran to the tower and climbed it anyway. It was Sgt. Brady, and we weren't about to leave him up there alone with all he'd done for us. When he saw our heads rising over the side, he pulled himself up, looked at us, and yelled "You two men, get the hell off this tower!"

We hung there, looking at him. We couldn't leave Sgt. Brady there. His voice grew angrier. "That's an order, damn it! You can't get me down! Leave me! Do it now! Go for the south road!"

I couldn't stand it. There we were, within arm's reach, but it was finally coming to me that he was right. There was no way we could get him down when he couldn't stand on the rungs. I lost my impetus, and took a backward step. Red followed my lead. Sgt. Brady knew he was as good as dead, and we knew it, too. Bullets whizzed past our heads. He wanted us to try to save ourselves. Since that's what he wanted, had ordered, we descended at his command, and left. I couldn't see where I was going for the tears in my eyes.

"Good men," he hollered through that horn. That's the last thing I ever heard him say.

Dodging through the Japanese forces, I lost Red in the confusion. I didn't even know he was gone until I said, "Red, I think I see a hole we can get through," and he didn't answer me. I looked around, but there were too many running men in uniforms, too much noise of battle, too much dust, too many dead—I couldn't see him anywhere.

I made it to the south road and started to make my way west toward Malinta Tunnel. Healthy and wounded men alike stumbled toward the tunnel, past bodies of the dead and maimed that lay everywhere. I saw a vehicle coming toward me that looked like a mini tank. I don't know for sure, but it was some kind of Japanese vehicle. I lay down in the shallow gutter and prayed fast. About that time, the thing ran over me. Once it passed, I shook, looked myself over, and felt OK. The driver must have gotten one wheel on the "curb," because the tank ran right over top of me.

I had been taught to crawl close to the ground, especially when in enemy territory. Maybe I had learned well, or maybe that was a deep gutter, or maybe the vehicle used to run me down had a high clearance underneath, or maybe God just had something else for me to do. At any rate, I lived.

I was still making my way toward the tunnel when I saw a large group of Americans being herded off to the south side of the road by the Japanese. There was an open space down there and maybe safety. I chose that way out, but somewhere during that time, a small piece of shrapnel lodged in my back. I didn't feel anything then—maybe my adrenaline was so high it would have had to take my leg off for me to notice. However, other guys had told me when small shrapnel first hits you, you don't feel it.

The Japanese soldiers were faceless to me, as I was to them. I came up to the crowd with my hands up, and blended in. They shoved us along with their rifles until we were where they wanted us to be. No announcements were made. They left a couple of guards, and the rest of them went off to finish taking Corregidor.

Down in that open space, I dropped onto the ground, my entire body and mind spent. All we could do was sit or lie down and wait, and I went nearly numb. Some of the others pulled their helmets over their eyes, put their arms around the backs of their heads, leaned forward, and seemed to sleep.

The war raged around us. After they had Monkey Point, the Japanese took charge of Malinta Tunnel, and then advanced on the larger portion of Corregidor. Machine guns, rifles, and bombs went off all afternoon, all night, and until noon on May 6, when General Wainwright officially surrendered the Rock. So went the fall of the USAFFE, the United States Armed Forces of the Far East.

This was real and unforgettable. I want to say we had given all we had. Then I think of those brave men who lay scattered across Monkey Point. Hundreds of men, like Sergeant Brady, and I guessed maybe Red. They had given a lot more. They had truly given all they had. Those of us who lay around the area for captives could still feel our pains. We could still hear the firing of guns as those Japanese overran the rest of Corregidor. At least we could still do that.

I am thankful for the blessing of not having to personally witness, as General Wainwright did, the Japanese pulling down Old Glory from Top Side's flagpole and trampling her under their dirty boots. I didn't have to see them run up their white sheet with a large red circle in the center.

I lay exhausted in this relatively quiet area of Monkey Point. No guards watched us. They were busy taking Topside. They figured we weren't going anywhere, and they were right. There was no battle left to fight, and so we rested. Only not knowing what would happen next kept any of us awake after all those hours of battle. We could hear gunfire in the distance, and I could just as truthfully use "we" for "I," because we all shared the same general situation. We had fired all our ammo, and we had left a few dead Japanese soldiers lying among those American heroes of Monkey Point.

We had no guns, no food, no clothes except what we were wearing. I, as well as most others, had not been to our barracks for five long months. Though we hated it, had fought against it all those months, depending upon someone else was now our only option.

That afternoon, American medics from the tunnel hospital were allowed to come out with first aid. They took care of some aches and pains, but not all. One dressed the spot on my back where the shrapnel entered, put some salve and a patch over it. It burned and hurt a while, and then settled down, so I forgot about it for about five years.

More Americans came out with blankets. We received one each as we lay there, wondering what would happen next. We had not slept in days and we were bone tired. It seemed about the right time to take a nap. At least one of us succumbed to sleep.

It was dark when I was awakened about twelve hours later by the commotion around me. The Japanese had allowed us at least one large pot of real nice soup mix. The commotion was because most of us had not eaten in at least twenty-four hours, and that soup tasted real good. Another thing we had learned in boot camp comes to mind. I did not hear one guy cry out, "What do you expect me to use to eat with?" We all had learned to hang onto our canteens, aluminum mess kits—the knives, forks, and spoons, along with our canteen cups. At least we were ready to eat. Our guys couldn't serve soup fast enough.

For the next three or four days, we had very little

supervision or attention. In fact, the only time anyone came around was when the soup kettle was brought out. We began to wonder if that was it. We would just sit there for no telling how long. Would the Japs line us up and shoot us, or what? Since there was no telling, I had two options: worry myself into suicide, or rest. I chose to rest.

Later, I learned that it was not until May 9 that the Japanese had full surrender from all US forces in the Philippine Islands. Those on the southern island of Mindanao had held on. I also learned later that we had about 11,500 Americans left on Corregidor after suffering 2,000 casualties. The total casualties for defending the Philippines, I am told, were about 140,000. A lot of those Filipinos also lost their lives.

I don't know the date, but before long, we saw an old ship pull close to the south shore of Monkey Point. We were hustled up, put on dinghies, and taken out there. We were not told anything, so no one had any idea where we were going, or why.

---

[1] "A G.I.'s Combat Chronology, Pacific 1941–1945," *VFW Magazine*, September 1995, p. 14–15.

What I Didn't Know—1

(US fortunes of war, May–November 1942)

I HAD NO INFORMATION ON THE BATTLES OF WORLD WAR II IN the Pacific when we began fighting the Japanese onslaught on Corregidor, after we were captured, or until I found myself in Camp Aomi in northern Japan, where we had a radio. I didn't even know the huge numbers captured. I had no idea that 11,500 Americans surrendered on Corregidor and another 12,000 on Bataan—a total of 23,500 POWs. That means of the approximately 28,000 Americans in the Philippines at the time, 4,500 had already been casualties of the war. It would be a lot later when we would know that of those 23,500 POWs, only 6,000 would return to the States, some having fallen on the Bataan Death March, some at Camp O'Donnell or the Cabanatuan camps. These are only the numbers from the Philippine theatre. Gavan Daws, in *Prisoners of the Japanese*, makes the point that the Germans only killed four percent of their POWs, while the Japanese killed twenty-seven percent. Linda Goetz Holmes says the more accurate

Japanese statistic is thirty-eight percent. The Japanese had hit nearly the whole string of fronts in the Pacific, and everywhere they landed, they took prisoners.

I also didn't know that on April 18, 1942, Jimmy Doolittle led his pilots in an air raid on Tokyo from a carrier task force, then landed in China. I didn't know this brave operation led Japan to overreact, sending every warship available to sea, generating a great deal of radio traffic. It was after the war when I read that this gave the US a tremendous opportunity to break Japanese codes and gather intelligence that changed the outcome of the war.

Our 1942 victories—in May in the Coral Sea, and June at Midway—were reframed by the Japanese and spewed at us POWs as defeats. Bull Halsey's August through November battles, resulting in eventual victory at Guadalcanal, were not known in the jungles of the Philippines or in Japanese POW camps. Even New Guinea was being won from the Japanese without us having any idea. In fact, there were many more battles less famous, fought by brave soldiers and sailors—yet we were told we were losing the war pitifully.

Manila, Underground, and the Freight into Hell
May–November 1942

THE NEXT MORNING, ALL CAPTURED ON CORREGIDOR WERE hauled close to the shore off Manila. The POWs waded to the beach and were paraded up Dewey Boulevard, the main street of Manila, toward the palace, so the Japanese could show off their strength and pride. Several Filipinos lined the boulevard as we walked along prodded by uniformed Japanese soldiers whose ball caps looked like someone had cut off half the visors.

The Filipinos looked like they had about as much enthusiasm for a parade as we had. Of course, the enemy soldiers among them probably "encouraged" them to stand and watch, the same way they were encouraging us to join the parade. I didn't know anyone around me, so I walked as directed. What else was there to do?

We walked a long way up the boulevard, turned a couple of times, and finally came to Bilibid Prison, where they penned us up. It seemed a little strange that the Japanese had not counted our numbers. Neither had anyone asked my name, rank, or serial number. I'd always expected that to happen when soldiers were captured.

We were herded into the backyard of Bilibid Prison, I presume for the night. I started looking through the crowd for my close buddies in the Special Duty squad. I found Joe, Casey, Hard Nose and Parks, who were also looking for me, but we couldn't find Red. I'd lost my partner. He must have been left out there among those 1,200 heroes who did not make the cut. We'd seen Col. Can Do come into the prison, but he was kept with the executive officer group.

Sometime after dark, the guards brought a large container of rice soup for our meal. That's about all we saw of them. The Japanese were not interested in what we were doing. I suppose those guys had their own agenda. There were no Filipino prisoners still in the prison—someone had let everyone go, or something. Hunkered over our mess kits, we began discussing our options with each other.

"There are no working guards around this prison, other than those Japanese who brought us up here. They're not interested in us," Hard Nose said.

"We could wait for someone to tell us what to do," Parks put in, "but I don't think we'll like what we hear. All I know is, I want out of here. The sooner the better."

"We could see what the back side of this prison looks like," Casey offered.

That nine- or ten-foot wall was a cinch for the first three. We stood next to it with four locked hands for a step. The end of a side arm belt served the other two. We had learned that maneuver in our Special Duty boot camp. At landing, we were looking at the *outside* of that high stone wall.

First, we ran across an open field, then through residential areas with clapboard houses. These neighborhoods were good for us, because the Filipinos appreciated Americans. They also hated the Japanese, so Japanese soldiers steered clear of residential areas. We looked at the stars and headed northwest, because we knew a highway and a railroad both headed north. We could get into trouble fast going through the main coastal area or to the south; the Japanese were fully concentrated there.

The next hours of daylight, we had to lay low because we were still too close to Manila. However, we had already located our highway and railroad. Most of us had ridden freight trains during the Depression. When we figured out where to catch our train, we only needed to wait until one came along and do once again what we'd done scores of times. Their railroad at that time ran steam engines on a narrow gauge. We easily caught our boxcar and rode the rails north.

Things went well until we reached Cabanatuan, in the north central valley. A large concentration of Japanese was encamped among the rice fields, so we could not stay on the train. When we began to see this, all five of us jumped into a squishy marsh of a rice field and silently made our way in the opposite direction from the enemy troops.

We later learned from Filipinos that three POW camps lay east of town, with the infamous Camp O'Donnell, where so many heroes of Bataan died, southwest of town quite a ways. Cabanatuan #1 and #2 were spillover from O'Donnell, for the guys who were already sick and dying. These two camps both sat in rice paddy country—lots of water and even more mosquitoes. The Japanese were building Cabanatuan #3 about twenty kilometers east of Cabanatuan, the town, and up into the foothills of the eastern coastal mountains. While we were there, they started work details of POWs from Cabanatuan #3 after the guys from Corregidor were brought in. Our guys were in much better health, it seemed, than those captured on Bataan.

The unit drifted north and west of Cabanatuan, through country with hills and mountains, and lots of country Filipino barrios. The people lived in bamboo shacks on stilts. The unit had discussed what we were to do now, and decided to help them resist the Japanese, if they were willing. Moving from place to place, eating off the land, we began to make friends.

Within a few days, we met Filipinos who had deserted the army as the Japanese overran Bataan. They had ditched their uniforms, changing into the shorts and pullover shirts of civilians in the tropics, then made their way through the jungle back to their homes in the northern countryside. Finally, some of them brought us to Domingo, their leader, who explained, "We want to set up a Philippine underground against Japanese, but need a little, a few ideas to get an operation started."

Joe said, "Hey, have we got ideas!" Making a motorcycle roar of a sound, he turned to us and said, "And I'm up for staying with these guys. It's safe here, and we can pretty well feed ourselves with what grows wild."

I thought about how we'd already been staying alive by eating rice and papaya as well as the other fruits that grew wild in the jungle. Mangoes and exotic fruit I didn't even know the names of hung from trees. We could probably add meat and Filipino delicacies from the people in the barrios.

We all assented with a nod, another situation where we assessed our options and chose to use what we had. While moving our position daily to avoid detection by any

Japanese spies who might be about, we began to explore what a good project might be.

They told us the Japanese were using Lingayen Gulf as the landing point for their supplies, just as they had their troops. The enemy trucked the supplies through the mountains to where they needed them, around Manila and central Luzon. When the trucks would start up the mountain, they slowed to a crawl.

We developed a simple plan in which we stopped the trucks on the mountainside. We walked out into the road, where they had to stop or run us down. The small Filipino men would hide in the green of the jungle that grew out over the highway, and once we'd stopped them, the Filipinos would swing out of the trees onto the trucks. They had bolo knives, about two to three feet long and as sharp as a razor. Screaming as they landed, the Filipinos would cleanly lop off the heads of the Japanese in the cabs of the trucks with their bolos. Those little guys loved taking revenge for Bataan. When they'd get back to the barrio, they'd spend hours telling each other and their women stories about the conquests of each day.

Before long, the American POWs from Cabanatuan #3 began driving trucks for the Japanese on work details. That made our job much easier. The POWs would stop the truck for us when the attack occurred. We didn't even need to walk out in the road anymore. They knew they would not be harmed. Besides, they got their own brand of revenge hauling the dead Japanese guards back to camp. The supplies the Filipinos lifted from the trucks brought good money on the black market.

We spent the summer of 1942 with the Philippine resistance. However, all good times must come to an end.

One evening Parks began to shudder and abruptly sat on a log. "I think I'm sick," he said. He was sweating and got weaker as the night wore on. His fever raged, he cussed and moaned. We didn't know how high his fever got because we had no thermometer, but he felt hot anywhere on his body we touched him. We had seen malaria plenty of times before, and we knew Parks had it.

"Please, get me something, do something," he begged when he was lucid. He rolled around on the mat. We couldn't let him suffer like that.

Folks used quinine over there at that time to cure malaria. Our Philippine country folk had no quinine, and getting it for Parks meant us going into town. Our big mistake was returning to Cabanatuan to "procure" the quinine. That place was a hotbed of enemy soldiers. Old Parks was extremely sick. We couldn't leave him with the Filipinos. If a Japanese patrol had happened on the Filipinos with Parks there, they would have killed everyone in the village.

Because of Parks' illness, we couldn't move very fast. As we snuck slowly toward the medic station, two Japanese soldiers came around a corner, and we were caught—prisoners of war (POWs) again.

We still had a little luck on our side, though. They had not taken our names, ranks, and serial numbers, so they had no record of prisoners escaping. To appear as innocent as possible, we had to be quick at thinking up a story to tell them. There was no interpreter at their post in town, so we couldn't talk to the Japanese and they couldn't understand us.

They walked us east, and soon we came to Cabanatuan POW Camp #1, where I got my first look at a Japanese POW camp. What a horror! It was located on a side road, just off the east/west thoroughfare. The enemy had posted two Filipino severed heads, one on either post, at the front gate. Some kind of depraved warning, I guess. Then a detail of live American skeletons stumbled toward us, carrying dead American skeletons out to a mass grave. No one spoke—not us, not them. None of them looked at us. No blanket or box covered the dead, no respect—just do it, the order of the day. It was walking death. I wanted to throw up.

I suppose the Japanese walked us out there because Camp #1 had an interpreter. They questioned us at length. Our yarn was that we were innocent boys caught up in this unfriendly war. We were lovers, not fighters. I am sure they did not like what they heard.

So what—I'd had about enough of them, too.

We began our journey once again, going east on the main road. Soon we walked by Cabanatuan POW Camp #2. We saw no heads on the gateposts, and we did not stop. Only I couldn't resist it. I hollered to a guy I thought looked a little like Red. Swiftly I received a blow in the ribs and high-pitched Japanese cussing. The Japanese did not put up with talking between POWs. The guy I'd yelled to didn't even look up. Like Camp #1, only a barbed wire fence encircled this camp. Those poor, starving, sick, and dying souls didn't have the strength to go anyplace very soon. There was no need for security.

About twenty kilometers out, we came to a secure-looking Camp #3. These guys looked much healthier. They probably had not been there as long, as most came from Corregidor or the southern islands. I guess the Japanese brought us out there because they planned for us to stay for a while.

We were taken into the guardhouse of the camp. Still they had not asked for our names, ranks, or serial numbers. We did not speak to any of the prisoners, even though they seemed curious. We'd all learned from my mistake that talking had serious consequences in prison camps. The prisoners were not permitted to come close to us.

The Japanese talked awhile. Then they held a kangaroo court for us. They lined us up and questioned us again. Of course they believed *every word* we said....

Finally, they decided we should be punished. They shoved us out behind the guardhouse and made each of us dig our own shallow grave. After we dug those graves, they brought out stools. Each of us was ordered upon a stool and given a stick to hold above our heads. If you think it must have been a large stick to be hard to do, try it some time. Without food or water, we stood in full view of the whole camp, with no hope of rescue except those graves. I guess the Japanese wanted to make the point that escaping had negative consequences.

For me, it became mind over matter as the night wore on. Everything in me hurt at first, and then slowly went dead. No talking was allowed, so I spent the time muttering or only thinking in military slang (better known as cussing) about those Japanese. Two guards, rifles in hand, stood waiting for any one of us to fall so they could shoot him. I had made up my mind to keep my life, but poor old Parks was too sick. His strength could not hold out. He turned to look at Joe, said, "I'm sorry I dragged you all back into this," and dropped his stick. We could do nothing but watch as they shot him and then left him lying there. Those guards represented the "yellow trash" of the Japanese people.

Morning finally came, and the four of us still stood. The guards changed, talked awhile, and we still hung on. That afternoon, the officer in charge came out. He gave the order to take us down. They pushed us off the stools, and somehow, though we were all stiff to the point of breaking, we managed to stay standing. If any of us had fallen, I felt sure we'd have joined Parks.

In a situation like that, a person can choose one of two things: laugh or cry. If you choose to cry, you will die, no doubt about it. So, when we could laugh, we did. We never cried. Feeling sorry for yourself was a luxury that cost many a man his life in Japanese captivity. I had to refuse to feel, and over time I got pretty good at it. Allowing no feeling has serious consequences, though. When I refused to feel anything about the horror around me, I also lost the ability to feel about good things I might have liked to enjoy. I even had to leave off thinking about home. Feelings are feelings, and POWs couldn't afford the luxury.

When they took us off the stools, we were put on a truck and returned to Cabanatuan, not knowing why or where we were headed. The Japanese were masters at keeping captives off balance and making sure we knew we did not matter to them. Sometime that night, we boarded a train for Manila. We still did not know where we were going or what would happen when we got there, and they still had not asked for our names, ranks, and serial numbers. This all happened about November 1, 1942—maybe the last few days in October. When we arrived in Manila, we were taken to the dock area on the bay.

Out in Manila Bay lay a rusty old freighter-type ship. They dumped us in a dinghy and took us out to that ship. That's as far as the four of us got to stay together. I was put in the front hold of the ship. Joe, Casey, and Hard Nose were taken to other portions. That old ship could have been one of those Japan had purchased from the US for scrap metal—nothing more than a piece of junk. I never learned its name. In the front cargo hold, they'd built a wooden frame inside the hull with horizontal shelves made out of plywood about every five feet that all met a vertical square hole in the center. One wooden ladder descended each side of the square hole for us to climb up and down to reach our shelves. Some light bulbs had been strung through each shelf.

Those Japanese may have fit well enough in a five-foot, floor-to-ceiling space, but for most Americans, it meant we had to crawl, rather than walk, to whatever position we could occupy on a shelf. Men were already fighting for position, the strong winning out over the weak.

The ship was already loaded with POWs when we arrived. I found myself on the portion of a shelf close to the square opening. I don't know how many men were on my shelf, but I'd guess more than a hundred. There was nothing to sleep on but the bare wood of the shelf. Some of the guys had more stuff around them than others. I still had my one blanket, side-arm belt and mess kit, knife, fork, spoon, and canteen, but I'd have to fight to keep them.

Someone told me we were headed for Japan. If I had allowed myself to feel, which I didn't, I'd have felt so hopeless and alone, it wouldn't have mattered anymore where I was headed. Assessing my options and using what I had wouldn't work in *this* hell-hole. I took my position and hunkered down.

Sometime that night, the ship lifted anchor and we set sail. The engine chugging and the ship vibrating rattled our teeth constantly, even in the front of the ship. I did not get to see Corregidor when we passed. The ship had no portholes, and we were not permitted on deck.

Somewhere in the China Sea, we met up with other freighter-type ships escorted by destroyers sailing around the perimeter for protection. I had the opportunity to see this when I was up on deck doing KP. We POWs didn't know it then, but there were US submarines plying that area of the China Sea at that time in the war. Because our ships weren't marked as transporting POWs, some of them were sunk, but not the one I was on.

I am told the water of the North China Sea is always rough. I know it rolled mightily on that trip, because nothing lowered down to us stayed in its container. Soldiers were seasick everywhere. It was cold near the opening in our hold—lots of mist and sometimes rain. Now and then the guards would cover the top of our hold. They never came down where they'd put us.

On the other hand, those guys on the back of the deck, next to the hull of the ship, really had a problem. They complained about the heat and lack of air to breathe. It could get extremely hot back there. After a few days, things began to get a whole lot worse. There was no clean-up detail.

We were fed rice twice a day. The Japanese would choose KPs from each section of each deck, one of the only times they talked to us. I tried to be on KP whenever I could, so I could get out of that hole at least for a little while. My position close to the ladder gave me a good start. I could race up the ladder against the other guys who tried. Every now and then I'd be first, and the guards let me climb out, go to the galley (kitchen), get the rice containers (thirty-gallon metal buckets), bring them back, and let them down to my section on a rope. I always took my time, breathing deeply, and got my scoop first, complete with bugs, eating in the fresh air.

By doing this I missed the action down at my section, where the idea was that the men would take the rice one dip per man. However, the reality was that if a man lay too sick to come to the opening, he starved. If one man was bigger and tougher than the man next to him, the other man starved. The can would hit the deck and the brutes would slam the weak out of the way, and growl and tear at each other until the container was empty. The empty container would be put on the rope, and I would lift it out.

We followed about the same procedure for drinking water. Whoever was KP would let the large container down on a rope. One drink per man was allowed. Some guys would always try to cheat. Soldiers fought like dogs, whether for water or rice. KP was no place to win friends.

The body-waste problem made a stinking, nasty proposition at best. They dangled a large can on a rope. Men would use the thing. It was all we had. Then they lifted the can on that same rope. Think now what that would be like, with thirty-foot swells. The men dumped it over the side of the ship. Those Japanese were not interested in cleanliness and taking care of the ocean.

For twenty-three days this continued. It does not take a lot of brains to realize this was a literal Hell Ship. Dysentery raged among the men. No one had a bath for twenty-three days. When someone died, his body was shoved out of the way, but not removed. With all this to live in, we knew that if we didn't fight to stay alive, we would join the dead. They forced us to live like nothing more than animals—survival of the fittest, and this against our buddies, the men we'd fought beside.

A few days out, just off Formosa (now Taiwan), we were the target of one of those US submarines I mentioned. The Japanese controlled Formosa at that time. The attack happened about rice-time one afternoon. I was on KP and on deck when the alarms began to sound. Everyone began running here and there—I just ducked down behind some kind of equipment, and no one noticed me. After a while, the "all clear" signaled. Atop one of those thirty-foot swells, I saw a destroyer in the distance. I saw smoke, so they had a problem.

That night we had our rice, but the convoy decided to pull into the Taipei harbor, where we anchored, sealed off from the China Sea. We spent a couple of days there, then pulled back out to sea and headed north toward Japan.

I don't know how some of those guys made it, if they did. The farther north we went, the worse things got in our hold. I am sure it was not any better in any of those other holds. When men continued to die, they were left in our hold rather than their bodies being thrown overboard, and the reek was unbearable. I guess the Japanese burned their bodies when they reached Japan.

We landed at Osaka, Japan, sometime in late November 1942—I believe about the time of our Thanksgiving. I was relieved to be off that Hell ship. About November 1, 1942, I had been in pretty good shape, health-wise and physically speaking. Three or four weeks later, I arrived in Osaka on the verge of death. I had gotten dysentery—along with I don't know what else—like the rest of the men. When I left Manila, in the tropics, I wore clothes designed for tropical weather. My physical system had been used to tropical living conditions for almost two years. One month later, I found myself in the winter weather of Japan still dressed in tropical clothes. This young man was sick, period.

Hopeless Guest of the Imperial Emperor of Japan
Thanksgiving 1942

THE MORNING WE WERE UNLOADED IN OSAKA, THE FOG rolled over the city, obscuring the view. I somehow found the strength to haul myself out of that reeking hole one more time. I wore a thin, short-sleeve shirt and G.I.-issue khaki pants into what must have been forty- or fifty-degree November weather. I had no shoes—only the sandals we had used in the Philippines. The cold air covered me with goosebumps, but it was also fresh. I took a deep breath and exhaled hard to try to remove the smell of death from my lungs.

The guards again marched us en masse up the main street, this time Osaka rather than Manila, in a victory parade for the few Japanese citizens who happened to be on the street at the time. The further away we got from that Hell ship, the better the air smelled. Sick and exhausted, I still breathed as deeply as I could of that fresh air while we dragged ourselves along. How long or how far we walked, I don't know, but late that afternoon we finally arrived at a camp they called Tanagawa. It was across the neck of the bay from Osaka. They informed us we were "guests" of the Imperial Emperor of Japan. I wondered why they didn't just say we were POWs, but I later found out why.

At Tanagawa, we had the typical military two-story clapboard barracks. In each one they had built double-deck shelving for prisoners to sleep on. An aisle ran down the center of the building. Each man was given a straw mat, which we laid side by side on the shelf—our heads to the aisle and our feet to the wall. We seemed to be the first shipment to that camp. At least, it appeared to me a learning experience for everyone, because the Japanese had no procedures in place, and *we* sure had no idea what we were doing! I don't recall lying down on my mat, but I did still have my blanket. It was dirty, but warmer than winter air.

The next morning, I could not stand up. I had a high fever with what felt like pneumonia. When a guard came through our barracks and saw that I was still on my mat, he had me taken to what was loosely termed the camp hospital. There was one room with, I think, eight straw mats on the floor. I was given one of them. Our heads were to one wall, with the walk space at our feet. There were no American doctors in our group of POWs. The Japanese gave no medication to anyone.

As for me, I had lost all hope. I was sick. I wanted to die. One last time I let myself look back in my mind to the scenes of my family enjoying dinner around our table, the expanse of the plains, football games at the high school, even the cotton gin—all the things of my past that would not be part of my future. It didn't matter that it made me feel totally lost and forgotten—I was going to die.

Nothing mattered anymore except getting out of this prison camp in the only way I knew. I was in another world, beat down by a foreign people who hated me. Maybe I was delirious; I don't know.

As I said, there was no medication at all, though I think I recall them bringing in rice soup. I lay there thinking all that day and the next night, while the others moaned and shifted on their mats. How could God let so many of us suffer this way? *Where are You?* I thundered in my head. *What could we have done to cause You to turn Your back on us like this?*

I thought back over the brave men I'd known, and all that happened on Corregidor, and imagined that I knew exactly when my mother had been praying for me, like when that tank didn't kill me. I wondered about Red—if I'd ever see him again, or whether he lay somewhere on Monkey Point. I wondered if the Japanese had buried Sergeant Brady. I'd seen all of the inhumane treatment I ever wanted to see, and yet my mind couldn't put it down.

The next afternoon, late, an old Japanese doctor came in. He was dressed in civilian clothes and had a couple of guards with him. He could speak English, so he talked to the POWs. I watched him examine each man in the way a doctor usually does, but all he had was heart—no medication.

"How many days on the ship?" he asked the guy closest to the door while he listened to his chest.

"Twenty-three," the feeble answer came. The doctor made no response as he continued his examination.

"You drink as much water as you can," the doctor ordered. He told the guards something in Japanese. They left, and he moved on to the next man. The guards returned, with a bucket of water with a dipper in it, and sat it next to the man by the door. *Water!* I thought—*the best you've got is water!* So the examinations went, until he came to me.

"How are you?" he asked.

I didn't answer. I didn't care. I didn't need him.

He began to examine me. I just lay there.

"You feeling very sick, huh?" he said.

"Humph!" I replied. The Japanese put me in this position, and I wasn't about to get chummy with any of them.

The doctor took a long look at me, then turned and spoke to the guards. They left and quickly returned with a pine box coffin—one like you see in the movies from time to time. It was set on its end in the corner.

When the doctor started to leave, I asked him, "Who is that for?"

He replied, "You, in the morning." Then he walked out.

That phrase. I felt like I'd undergone a direct hit from one of those bombs on Monkey Point. Until then, I had lost hope, no doubt about it. I had wanted to die. Have you ever looked death in the eye? I mean, face-to-face? The guy next to me was lying stone still, but looking at me. Looking at me like he thought I was dead already. He sure looked like he was going to accompany me, if that were the case. At any rate, I looked at that pine coffin all night long.

I thought, *so, Baker, it's for you. You ready to die? You dead already?* As I stared, the coffin grew larger, some kind of optical illusion in my delirium. I always thought I'd have a big funeral, with one of those coffins with handles, and all my relatives would carry me out to the graveyard. I always thought I'd live to have children and later watch my grandchildren play in my yard, like my grandparents' grandchildren had. That was all supposed to happen before I died. The night wore on, but I couldn't sleep.

Sometime in the early morning, I thought, *maybe I might be able to survive. What if the United States wins this war and frees those of us left here? I don't want to have died for nothing but that cursed Hell ship. I want to be one of those alive when the Americans come to free us. It doesn't matter that there's no medicine, or that I'm sicker than I've ever been.* Then some of those Sunday-school stories I heard as a kid started to filter through my brain. I thought, *God knows I'm here. People throughout history have suffered, but God was still with them. He eventually saved them. He saved the Israelites in Egypt by giving them Moses to lead them. God hasn't forgotten us, either. Maybe there's a Moses here. I want to let God do with my life as He sees fit, not just take it upon myself to let it go. Nobody is able to take me from God—not the Japanese, not anybody, no matter what they do to me. I'll tell myself that when I need to. I am not ready to go out of this life in that box.*

I felt a little stronger. *What are my options? I could lie here and be dead tomorrow, but that's out. I'm going to live. I can use what I have. When the sun comes up, I'll get up off this mat and out of this place.*

I got what I like to call a "hope transplant" that night. Nothing had really changed—I was still a POW with no idea what was coming, when or if I would be released, or whether the Japanese or the United States and our allies might win the war. My prospects for the immediate future were bleak. Only there were angels watching over my thoughts and me that night. Maybe one of them was that old Japanese doctor—I don't know. I never saw him in the camp again. The next morning, this old boy went back to my barracks.

I was not physically well, but I had hope. When we know for sure what hope is and where it comes from, then hope is all we need to succeed.

What *is* hope? "Hope is our confident desire for something with a definite expectation of receiving it." I had memorized a part of that little red-letter New Testament the Gideons gave me. Hebrews 11:1 says, *"Now faith is the substance of things hoped for, the evidence of things not seen."* I could not see those things I hoped for, but my faith in God gave me strength to know in my heart I would see them.

Through it all, what had already happened, and what was to come, Jesus was with me. I assure you He is God, and He is powerful. He is powerful enough to turn a prisoner of war who was ready to pack it in away from suicidal thoughts toward hope for his life.

Slave of the Imperial Emperor of Japan

December 1942

BACK AT THE BARRACKS, WE HAD A LOT OF LEARNING TO DO—how to speak Japanese, for instance. The first language lesson I remember was learning to count in Japanese. Those numbers go something like this: *itchey, nee, san, yan, go, roko, nana, hatchey, ku, ju*. Then you learn to combine the numbers to count further up the scale. Japanese is a hard language to learn, and for me, very easy to forget. As a POW, being battered for not getting your attempts right only addled the brain.

The first Japanese fellow I really got to know—and hate—was our camp interpreter. To hear him tell it, he was the main guy. I'll call him Hangnecker. At our first meeting, he let us know that he came from San Francisco, California, and he had inside information that the West Coast would be invaded any day by Japanese forces. He was one of those little banty-rooster–type guys who strutted around in his uniform, waving whatever he had in his hand at the time in the air, puffing out his chest, displaying all the importance he could muster.

Walking right up to our chins, he yelled, "The Japanese Navy has bombed and shelled California, Oregon, and Washington! You are pitiful wretches from a cowardly country that soon will belong to Japan!"

Apparently, it didn't take much to get his imagination in gear. History indicates that the closest his story came to truth was when a Japanese submarine shelled an oil refinery near Santa Barbara, California, on February 23, 1942. On June 22, another Japanese sub shelled Fort Stevens, Washington. Then on September 9, one light plane launched from a Japanese submarine dropped a small bomb near Brookings, Oregon. It started a forest fire. After that, all was quiet on America's western coast. However, to hear old Hangnecker tell it, the US was folding—we POWs may as well get used to Japanese customs and slavery.

My personal number was 383—*san yako hatchey ju san*. I had a terrible time learning it. Every time I failed, old Hangnecker would yell his amazement at how stupid Americans were, and hammer me with his fists or club me in the head with his sword of authority. He didn't help the learning process a bit.

As a matter of fact, he would pummel us out of the clear blue—it didn't have to be because we weren't learning fast enough, it could be for no reason at all. Hangnecker taught me that, though some folks fast and pray, what a POW needed to do was *pray fast*—especially when tyrants like Hangnecker were around. There wasn't time to consider what I might ask God for—I just silently cried out, "Stop this guy!"

What a fraud and traitor he was. He had escaped from the US on December 8, 1941—Pearl Harbor Day for me, along with the embassy personnel from San Francisco. They were allowed to leave unchecked. Thugs like Hangnecker scared the bureaucrats in Washington, D.C., and Sacramento, California, into thinking everyone with an Asian face was an enemy of the United States. The bureaucrats rounded up all the fine Japanese-American citizens—many who'd been born in the United States—and held them prisoner for the duration of the war. Those people had sons and daughters in service to our country. They themselves had worked to build the United States, just like the rest of us. What a shame.

Perhaps there had previously been a few bad guys among them, but untouched, the majority of the bad guys had left the country. At the end of the war, the war crimes tribunal in Tokyo rounded up about 6,000 Class B and C criminals like Hangnecker and brought them to trial. They sentenced about 3,000 and executed over 900. I still struggle with hoping Hangnecker died among that 900. He certainly earned an early death.

Japanese civilians were brought in to teach us the language. The few important words I recall are: *Honjo* (pronounced "honcho"), which means guard or boss; *Keasky* meant "attention"; *Biokey* meant "sick"; *Bango* meant "count off"; *Yasume* meant rest; *Doma* meant "no good"; *Hyaka* meant "hurry up"; *Joto* meant "OK" or "good."

At last, they confirmed or recorded our names, ranks, and serial numbers. I finally was given a wool British Army shirt and pants that helped me withstand the cold a little better.

Then the *Honjo* came onto the parade ground one day. We had counted off and stood at attention. Through Hangnecker, he said, "You are not POWs. Japan never signed the Geneva treaty; therefore, we have no need to tell anyone, including the Red Cross, that you are here. However, you will be required to write home, twenty-five words or less each week, to your next of kin; and because Japan is a fine country, we will mail your letter postage-free. You are guests of the Emperor of Japan." What he was telling us was that we were actually slave laborers for the Japanese. Our not technically being POWs relieved Japan of treating us well as the Geneva Convention dictated. Essentially, they could do whatever they wanted with us and to us. Brother!

When we wrote our letters, we could in no way tell our relatives our location or when any bad thing was wrong with us. We could only tell our folks that we were under the control of the Imperial Japanese Emperor and being treated fairly. I wrote my card to my mother each week I lived as a POW—132 cards in all, as best as I can count. I thought she would at least have the peace of knowing I was still alive.

We unloaded freight cars in a railroad switching yard on my first work detail. The whole thing was a new experience for the Japanese guards, civilians, and for the POWs. We looked at their slanted eyes, and they looked at our round ones. I wondered if they ever considered what kind of people would be living behind our eyes, like I did about them, if this hadn't been war.

Right then, the Japanese soldiers' eyes glared hard at us; they sneered at our cowardice for not choosing death instead of being captured, and pounded their chests about how they would never serve an enemy—they'd die first. The war was going in their favor at the time, so maybe they were justified, at least a little. The US was still rebuilding, and propaganda flowed freely in Japan. Those Japanese people believed what they heard.

I thought some about the honor of dying instead of slaving, but life is life, hope is hope. I'd already settled all that with God. There was honor in doing what it took to stay alive. I disagreed with the Japanese on that score as well as many others.

One particular morning, we were unloading straw sacks of rice from a railroad car and carrying it into a warehouse. A medium-sized dog came around looking for a scrap of food. Compared to later in my POW experience, we were being fed pretty well, because they had the food and expected us to work to earn it—but we were low on protein.

As the dog sniffed around our feet, looking for something we might have dropped, one of the Japanese guards said something in Japanese to a civilian worker, who roared with laughter. Pretty soon, guards and civilians were all discussing their hysterical idea, laughing and slapping their legs. Finally, one of the guards pointed with his rifle at the dog and made motions that meant eating to us. We were hungry, and meat was meat. All we'd had for days was rice. It did not take long for us Americans to return their joke.

One guy said, "Hey, if they'll furnish the rice, catch the dog, and kill it, we can cook and eat the stew. Of course, some of us will have to be off work for the cooking and cleaning. Too bad, huh?" We gestured all this back to them, and the Japanese took us up on the deal. The rifle roared and the dog's head came clear off. Though the experience was a first for all of us, the guards did have the presence of mind not to give us knives. The guards gutted and skinned the creature, and cut hunks off to throw in a huge pot they had us bring out from the camp. Two men were permitted to cook the dog, with plenty of good rice. The smell of that dog cooking set my mouth to watering. Those Japanese thought we were a real sideshow.

Word got around. When our work detail stopped to eat, we had a curious crowd of Japanese onlookers. There were little children and their parents, workers from nearby office buildings—even some older folks, who stood with canes, gazing at us as if we were part of a dog-and-pony act at the circus.

One of our guys, wiping broth from his chin, said, "Man, this is better than any deer I ever ate." Another, laughing with his mouth full, replied, "Tastes like chicken to me."

We ate and ate, filling our stomachs. The Japanese enjoyed the show, while about 100 or so hungry POWs actually had a real good meal of dog stew with rice. Everyone went back for seconds. Those angels who seemed to be hovering over Tanagawa managed to look out for a bunch of hungry American POWs with the gift of that dog.

It had been long enough since the Hell ship that most of the internees in our camp were well fed again. Those were the good times for Japan, so we ate rice, whale, squid, and in pretty good servings. The unusual foods fell just fine on this old Texas boy's stomach.

Unfortunately, we were about to find out that the Japanese weren't just being nice. We were to be human mules, and the Japanese fed us pretty well because they wanted us strong.

I Killed a Guard, Mom
January–February 1943

OUR FIRST WORK PROJECT AT TANAGAWA NEARLY KILLED US. We were digging a huge pit for a dry dock. I have never determined whether it was for a naval base repair project, or maybe just a shipbuilding operation. It really makes no difference—American and Korean slave labor accomplished the entire project, and I was one of them.

As I look back over sixty years of history and recall recent events, I can see how our slave labor may have played out. I study maps of modern Japan and see where we labored. I know what we did to change that part of the world. We filled in the top end on the neck of the bay between Osaka and Kobe, Japan, with the dirt that was the fruits of our labor. I also recall an earthquake in 1995, in Kobe, Japan. I saw pictures of that one-legged freeway lying over on its side. I cannot help but wonder whether it was built on the landfill I'd helped with.

We got up early each morning, ate our bowl of rice, and then worked at least ten hours per day. We had a day of rest, a *yasume* day, every once in a while, but not every week. When we came in from work in the evening, a charcoal burner—smaller than an average American barbecue grill—placed in the center aisle of our barracks served as a cruel reminder of the bitter cold.

We soon learned to share blankets and straw pads for warmth. Not that we liked sleeping with other men—we were just trying to survive a hard winter in a Japanese slave camp, while being listed as "guests" of the Imperial Emperor of Japan. I must classify him as my worst host, period. My blanket-partner was Dale, a younger soldier than I, from Iowa, and a fine person.

Narrow-gauge railroad tracks had been built on a framework of wood that stretched from the dry dock pit out over the neck of the bay. The Japanese would load train cars much like we use in our eastern US coal mines. Two POWs would push them on the track out over the bay, where they would be dumped.

We shoved those cars round and round all day long—winter and summer, rain or shine. I would watch that dirt fall into the sea and think to myself that each load was nothing to the sea—a mere piece of dust in the eye. How many men, striving through how many trips, would it take to hold back the sea?

We turned to skeletons, skin on bones, and still we labored. As we filled more of the bay, our captors would simply extend the tracks, and I would look moment by moment into the yawning mouth of the ocean that never got its fill of dirt.

Then came one of those *yasume* days. I had written my card to my mother and laundered my only suit of clothes, but a toothache I'd had for a while was worsening. My wisdom tooth on the right side had abscessed. Since there were no doctors or medical personnel at that camp, I went by the office to see if I could get pain pills or something.

Those Japanese guards listened to my complaint and saw a chance to do what they loved to do—make someone hurt. The guards in that camp were the worst I experienced. They seemed to love knocking your head off for no good reason. Most of the other "guests" and I were already black and blue, if not nursing broken ribs, from beatings the guards gave for sport.

Some of the guards ganged up on me. Two of them came to the barracks and dragged me out in the compound where everyone could see. They yelled and screamed at me as if I had planned the abscessed tooth. Several of them sat on me, laughing, while others gouged with knives and other tools and dug that tooth out.

My god—that was probably the most pain I have ever experienced at one time. Not one bit of Novocaine or even a pain pill. I tried to close my mouth, to bite them, but it was impossible. Those guys just listened to me gag and yell every time their hands were out of my mouth. My Sunday school teacher would have been red-faced if she had heard me, because I called those heathen guards everything I could think of—maybe something else even.

I had to jerk my head to the side and spit to keep from drowning in the blood coming from the root of the tooth, and that made them laugh harder. Once they had the tooth, they danced around, holding it up as if it were a gold medal. Then one of them ceremoniously put it in my pocket. They stood me up and kicked me toward the barracks.

That afternoon and night in the barracks, I hurt. My jaw swelled up, and the pain covered my whole head. Shutting my eyes was the only help, and even that only worked for a while. The guys in the barracks could do nothing for me. No one had any kind of medication. Every time a guard would come through, he would laugh, point at me, and tell another guard, who had missed it, about the experience.

However, it paid to have a close buddy. Since all my squad buddies had been sent someplace else, I had gotten to be good friends with the kid named Dale, my young blanket-partner from Iowa. I say "kid," because he was one of those eighteen-year-olds who had been caught up in the draft. During the times we could find to talk, he told me he was a farm boy. He told stories about his parents, and described things that happened in the little town where he lived. This was probably his first trip away from home. We had begun to work together on the project.

This night, once the sun went down and he could move without the guards spotting him, he took his shirt and folded it up. I saw the goose bumps break out on his skin as soon as he took it off. First, he held it to the burner to warm it, then brought it and laid it on my jaw. "Maybe this'll help a little," he whispered.

"Thanks," I replied, as the warmth did indeed slow the pain.

He slid back under our blankets, shivering, and said, "I think I remember that warmth only works for a while, and then you have to switch to cold. So, let me know when the warm ones stop working, OK?"

I nodded.

He brought hot pads and then cold pads, to try and help me stop hurting, all through that night. I think I even slept a little toward morning. Then they routed us out to our work detail, as usual.

A few days later, Dale and I were working out at the project, going up and down that long ramp pushing our tramcar full of dirt out over the bay, dumping the load, making the turn at the end of the track, and then back for another load. We were in the middle of this routine when we came upon a Japanese guard beating a young POW unmercifully. He'd stomp away from the boy for a little bit and then turn on him, yelling and screaming—you could hear his screeching a mile away—and hammer him with blows from his rifle butt. The young man was already down, bloody, not even holding his arms above himself as a shield from the guard's onslaught anymore. The guard was about to beat the poor kid to death.

We always had our heavy steel bars to dump our loaded tramcar. Our car came nearer and nearer along the track, closer to that yelling guard. He was strutting around there like a crazy man, but he always kept his eye on the kid he was beating. A sudden impulse entered my mind. I don't know what happened. I certainly did not assess my options.

We came close by, and without my giving it any thought, once we were within arm's reach, my heavy steel bar fell upon the guard's head with a sickening crack. It stopped his yelling and tore his head wide open. A little late, I thought to look for other guards, saw none, and with Dale's help, I quickly threw the guard into the bay. Dale never said a word, and he didn't help kill the guard, but he did help throw him in the bay. Bless his soul. Soon we had a lot of infill on top of the body. It felt as if the whole thing was over in a heartbeat.

I don't know what happened in my head that day. I acted without premeditation, and when it was over, even *I* was surprised. I never knew what happened to the POW the guard nearly killed. I never saw him after that. However, no one came around asking about the guard, so that kid didn't tell anyone about me, or if he did, he didn't know how to identify me.

I suppose that Japanese guard was the only man I ever intentionally killed who wasn't trying to kill me, but there was no time to contemplate my act. That poor kid should not have been beaten like that. I have said it before, and I'll say it again: war is hell. My conscience bothered me over killing the guard, even though he was killing that kid. After all, the guard wasn't *my* enemy. He was the boy's enemy. He wasn't like the pilots of those planes we shot down over Corregidor, who would try to kill us if we didn't kill them first. On Corregidor, it was war—an exchange. An evil exchange, but an exchange. With the guard, I took a life whether I intended to or not.

I asked God to forgive me. I believe He did. I think when I get to Heaven, I'll have to tell the truth about killing that guard, but when I'm through, I believe Jesus will pat my shoulder with His nail-scarred hand and tell me I am already forgiven. So, I ask you to forgive me also.

Then came another *yasume* day. Each time we had one, I was ready for a day away from that work project, where those Japanese guards would rather knock your head off than eat lunch, but this day was especially welcome. I had written my mother, almost as usual. This time, I wondered what she would think if she knew I had killed that guard. I didn't tell her, of course. That would have cooked my goose, since I assumed the Japanese read what we wrote, and it wasn't the kind of thing I'd write in a letter, anyway. Thinking about talking to her made my mind wander back. I wished I could talk to her.

I always felt those little prayers my mother prayed for me, even before I enlisted in the army. I was convinced in my heart that she was praying for me her little, important prayers that *yasume* day while I was a POW in a Japanese slave camp. They made me feel more like living again.

I loved my mother. She was the most important person in my life. If it were not for my mother, I wouldn't have survived being a POW to live the life I live today. I believe it's the same for most of us—our mothers are the most important people in our lives, and they watch over us whether they're alive or have already gone on.

At any rate, I wondered that day whether the florist at home had thought on Mother's Day to deliver the box of Whitman chocolates and the red rose I gave my mother each year, and whether she would remember on the next Mother's Day. I had intended to send the money for it, but I had not been able to. I just kind of wondered. It sure looked like the florist would have to do it on faith, and maybe for a while, if it were to get done—because I apparently wasn't going home anytime soon.

What I Didn't Know—2

(US fortunes of war, spring 1943)

DURING THE SPRING OF 1943, WHILE I WAS BUILDING THE DRY dock in Osaka Bay, Australian and British POWs in Burma and Siam were building two sections of a railroad that, if finished more quickly than it was, might have turned the tide of the land war in the Pacific for the Japanese. These men died at a rate of over 400 per mile. I'm glad I didn't know about them then.

During this time, there were victories and defeats for both sides, but the event I truly would have liked to know about was the death of Admiral Yamamoto, who had been responsible for Pearl Harbor as well as the attacks on the fronts across the Pacific. It seems that US intelligence was experiencing increasing success at breaking Japanese codes. One message they decrypted was Admiral Yamamoto's itinerary for a personal tour of airfields on Bougainville, Ballele, and Shortlands.

Admiral Nimitz, having consulted the President and the Secretary of the Navy, told Bull Halsey that if he had the capability to shoot down Yamamoto and his staff, he should do it. Major John Mitchell's squadron took on the assignment, and a year to the day after Doolittle's Tokyo raid, April 18, 1943, Japan lost their supreme naval admiral over Bougainville.

Another important event during this time was the meeting between Bull Halsey and General Douglas MacArthur, on April 15 in Brisbane. These two leaders, whose strong personalities were legendary, had some worried that if they were at odds, the war would be seriously affected. However, they liked each other immediately and planned a combined army/navy offensive for the rest of 1943.

Of course, none of this was told to POWs. The death of Yamamoto was even kept from the Japanese until his ashes had been brought home on a carrier. The information we were fed was that the Japanese were hammering the rest of the world to mush. At the same time, the Japanese were refusing to cooperate with the Red Cross. Thus, for many months, they issued no lists of POWs or death certificates to let any of our countries know our fate.

Rations and Tragedies
March 1943

AMERICANS WERE NOT THE ONLY EMACIATED SLAVES working up and down, around and around, digging the dry dock and filling the bay. Japan had already overrun Korea before taking the Philippines. There were Korean men who had been yanked up and brought to Japan for the sole purpose of slave labor. They were bigger than the Japanese, did extremely heavy work, and got nothing but their food. The Japanese saw them as tools that had to be fed. However, if they did not work, they did not eat.

One big, strong Korean slave, who worked on the project near where Dale and I went around and around, became sick. Though there were a large number of Koreans working on the dry dock, this huge Korean was the only one I know of who got sick. Even ill as he was, that poor guy still had to go to the bottom of the dry dock pit, have a large rock loaded into his backpack, and climb a ladder to the top of the wall frame to a work-scaffolding walkway. He then carried the stone to the place where the Japanese wanted it dropped into the cement they were pouring for the wall.

He trudged to the job more slowly each day, but finally could not carry the rock. Though he was a giant among Koreans, that day his disease made him too weak to make it up the ladder anymore. We happened to be at a place in our circuit where we could see him put his foot to the bottom step, attempt to lift the other foot, appear to bow slowly to the Japanese guard, and fall back into the pit with a grunt.

The Japanese guard started cursing, pulled the Korean's pack off, and heartlessly beat him. He gestured to us to drag him out of the pit with sign language that said no work, no food.

Several of us went down into the pit, and working together, managed to bring him out. His eyes had rolled up in his head, but he mumbled something to us that I assumed was a thanks. We laid him beside the track, and I rolled up my shirt under his head. Then we had to resume our circuit.

What a hoax to say he could not eat! The man would only get weaker. We felt sorry for him, so we hauled him back to the barracks at the end of the day, and some of us shared our rice rations with him to keep him from starving to death. The Japanese on that project were stonehearted, and we were forced to experience their inhumane treatment of human beings day after day. The big Korean did eventually recover and went back to work.

It's interesting that the camp conditions at Tanagawa paralleled the diminishing strength of the Japanese navy. Though we didn't know the Japanese were beginning to lose the war—in fact, were told the opposite daily—the rations of the men in Camp Tanagawa, Japan, were decreasing with each passing day. I imagine some of us guessed that our portions and their fortunes might be linked.

In January, February, and March 1943, the American Navy and Air Force were making serious gains against the Japanese forces in New Guinea, the Solomon Islands, and the Bismarck Sea. Our rations in camp had shrunk to 450 calories per day. *Anyone* will lose weight on 450 calories a day. I was down to somewhere near 100 pounds, from about 175. I had no scale, but when you can count all your ribs just by looking, it isn't tough to guess your weight. It wasn't just me, either. We all looked like that, skin and bones, and still worked like mules. Some of us managed to stay healthy, but those who succumbed to dysentery or beriberi died. A familiar face would miss count off one day and then disappear. I guess they went to that joke of a hospital and were carried off after they died.

Regardless of our emaciated state, we continued to move those tramcars of dirt and rock from the ever-growing maw of the dry dock pit to the ever-decreasing space of the bay. Weather was not a consideration. When it was hot, we sweated. When it rained, we were given a piece of straw mat to hang over our shoulders for a raincoat while we continued going around and around. Whatever the weather, I used the time to think about generally unimportant, useless things that came to mind. All the multiplication tables up through twelve, unusual words for all the letters of the alphabet, made-up Japanese cusswords to describe Japanese guards—whatever happened to float through to pass the time. I refused to think about things that mattered to me, like my family, Texas, continuing my life. Hope drained out when I let myself go there, so I didn't go.

One bleak, rainy day in March, Dale said to me as we pushed our tramcar out over that icy blue water, "I don't think I am going to make it." It had finally happened—he had lost all hope of ever getting out of there. I could see it in the way he held his head, his energy gone.

I reached over and cuffed him. A dangerous move, with so many guards around, but desperation shaded his eyes and I had to do something. "Naw, you'll make it. You've got to make it," I replied, trying to encourage him. "A guy who'll give up his shirt to help a guy with a sore tooth has got to make it." I grinned. He didn't.

After work, we went to camp as usual. We washed up a little in the cold water and ate our meager servings of rice and bugs. It was not long before we went to bed. That was the only way to get warm. I don't recall what we talked about. He probably talked about home. His homesickness never left him. I hope I told him all I knew that might have helped him regain his lost hope.

The next morning I woke up and turned to say something to Dale, but his face, which had always been fair complected, was now pale. He was dead. My young buddy, my friend, had given up.

"Aw, Dale!" I said. I got out from under our blankets and covered his head. It was all I could do. I couldn't cry. I cared, but in a place like Tanagawa, crying was a luxury not to be afforded. Crying diminished hope. I went about my morning routine, ate the rice the guards brought, and when I left the barracks, Dale was still lying there under our blankets.

For any POW, when hope was gone, death stepped in. That is how close death was to our weakened bodies. I'd had my hope transplant in November or December, because a fine Japanese doctor shocked me back into reality. Hope enabled me to endure the harsh treatment we all received working as slaves.

Young Dale couldn't—probably for many reasons—maintain his hope. Dale gave his practically innocent life, which he'd barely begun, for the sole purpose of helping the Japanese government build that enemy dry dock. It made me sick, but not sad. I couldn't afford to feel sad. When I came back to camp that night, our blankets were there, but his body was gone. I guess they cremated the boy. I wish I could have told his family how good he'd been to me and how much he loved them.

"You Are Not Supposed to Be Happy" April–August 1943

SPRING ARRIVED IN TANAGAWA. THOUGH THE SKY WAS finally blue and the sea sparkled, the gulls' cries seemed still to mourn our situation. Everyone was losing weight, but we were still expected to work as hard as ever. The Japanese soldiers were quick to yell down and knock around anyone who even acted like he wanted to move more slowly. They were determined to finish that project as soon as possible. I can't speak for all the POWs, but the ones I talked with at all had assessed our options and were determined to work as little as possible, chancing a beating now and then, since that's the only method we had at hand to help the US win the war. It was more tolerable to work in warm weather, though.

We were close to the finish line, as far as the dirt moving was concerned. Every POW there anticipated with glee the end of going around and around that track day after day after day.

Then, one day, we went to the barracks from work and

lined up for the count-off before being dismissed. Mr. Hangnecker climbed onto his announcing box and yelled, "We are having a *yasume* day. You are to clean up the barracks and the camp in general. If you do well, you have an extra *yasume* day. That is all." He jumped off his box, and walked into the headquarters building.

Two days in a row! What was wrong? Was the war over?

The war was far from over. No, they had called in a photographer, and we were to have individual pictures taken. For what reason, I had no idea. My turn came to go before the camera.

"Repeat your number!" Hangnecker yelled.

"*San yako hatchey ju san,*" I yelled. Then I sat on a stool with my back to the board fence around the camp. The picture shows that our diet didn't have enough vitamins in it to grow a beard, and I was beginning to lose my hair.

The woman photographer had an old-style camera sitting on a tripod, with a large black cover made of material in the back. She got under the cover to focus and take the picture, and to keep from exposing the film. Her camera was like the ones we see in movies about the Old West.

For a while, the photographer fiddled and fooled with the camera, trying to focus the thing just right, I suppose. Then she looked clear underneath the camera toward me. Naturally, the Japanese women have a round-type face, but this lady had on large, round, heavy eyeglasses. She looked like she was looking through the bottom of Coke bottles. I could not help but laugh out loud. There, gazing at me, was the funniest-looking face I had seen in a while. I can honestly say this was another time I did not assess my options. I would have laughed if it had killed me, and it nearly did.

Mr. Hangnecker ran over and yelled in my face, "You are not supposed to be happy!" Then—*wham*—he busted me in the head.

I picked myself up off the ground, head swimming.

"Get back on the stool, and get serious!" he screamed. In the picture, you can see a knot swelled out over my left eye from Hangnecker's rifle butt.

The photographer still looked funny, and I did get in a little grin, but I think part of that grin said, "I'll live, no matter what you do to me."

After the pictures were taken, I happened to be in the office where they were laid out on a table. I got a chance to get a copy of mine, and took it—a five-finger discount, so to speak. I managed to bring it home, about one inch square. It's enlarged, and you can see it here. The shirt I'm wearing is that wool British army shirt.

The latter part of July or the first of August 1943, we began to hear rumors that some of us would be moving north. That move may have been what the pictures were all about. Everything seemed to turn around those who were in the best health and physical condition. In other words, wherever we were going, they wanted only healthy men who could work. Healthy skeletons, but disease-free, nevertheless. We didn't know any more details. All we could do was sweat it out.

It wasn't long before they chose about 200 or so men. They told us to prepare to ship out the next day. It wasn't tough to pack—we didn't have suitcases—just pick up your blanket and your mess kit, and off to the train station we marched. We boarded a regular passenger train, with seats. One guy said, "Fellas, we are in the chips!" We had only ridden boxcars with nothing to sit on in the Philippines, and sometimes during the Depression in the States.

We traveled up the east coast of Japan, north of Tokyo, picking up about 200 more men from other camps along the way. We had about 400 POWs when we arrived at Aomi Camp in northern Japan. It was a mountainous region—different country than the coast we'd been used to in the Osaka area. I do not know if the small town was named Aomi or not, but that was the name of our camp. There was a rushing river in the canyon, along which ran railroad tracks until they left the river at a certain point. Uphill from the tracks was the small town, and then about halfway to the mountain's rugged summit was our camp. The mine was above the camp. The mountain's trees and wildflowers were beautiful, but a clear contrast to the tramped-out POW camp.

There had been about 600 British army men working the mine and smelter operation, but they were dying off too fast and needed to be replaced. We were those replacements. About 200 of the British men were kept there, making a total of 600 once we arrived. When I saw the mine up there on the mountain, I thought, *Here we go again. More human mule imitations, and more stalling and more beating. What fun.*

The barracks were about the same as those at Tanagawa. Each had two stories with a wooden shelf-like space on both floors, so they actually could sleep four floors of men in two stories, feet to the wall, head to the center aisle. The Japanese were masters at cramming a lot of men into small spaces. We had a little charcoal pot for heat, again no heat, but I still had my blanket. We used a binjo ditch outside the barracks for a bathroom, and hoped the wind blew away from our housing. Having lost Dale, and coming again to unfamiliar territory, I wondered if the Japanese purposely changed all our circumstances frequently to control us.

The makeup of the camp staff was a lot different. In Tanagawa, the staff had been Japanese army personnel. In Aomi, there were a *honjo* and guards who were army, a Japanese army colonel as camp commander, and Japanese soldiers who guarded the camp from the guardhouse at the camp front gate. The armed guards only lined us up, counted us off, and marched us to the front gate. The same procedure was repeated when we returned to camp. Inside the gate, we belonged to the army. We learned later that we were working for a Japanese corporation—Mitsui Mining Co.—rather than on a government work project this time. Those bossing the men outside the camp on work details were employees of Mitsui. We still got no pay, and our status as guests of the Imperial Emperor of Japan remained the same.

Our first formation was to receive our new number. My new number was 440, or *yanyako yan ju*—a lot easier to count off with. Then we were assigned to our barracks. I have described them already, but in Aomi, we had a long hallway with a lot of sinks with running water so we could wash up. Here we had a sort of recreation room, with some tables and chairs—a nice addition for a POW camp.

It wasn't long before I found out that we also were allowed to bathe in that crystal-blue river once a week. We'd march down there, cold weather or warm, strip, and jump into that icy mountain water. Notice I didn't say we stripped to skivvies—nobody had underwear anymore, so we didn't go for convention. None of us had soap, either, but a bath is a bath, and we rubbed what grime we could off with our hands. Sometimes we even got a little splashing in at some of the other guys. That guy on the train had been right—we really were in high cotton. I watched to see if I could find any of my old unit buddies when we went to the river or out on details, but I didn't see any faces I knew.

I heard through the rumor mill, during our first few weeks at Aomi, that American planes had bombed the dry dock at Osaka and the POWs still there had to start all over. Too bad for the Japanese, but way worse for the POWs. At least I didn't know yet what brand of poison they had in store for us here.

From Harley to Eternity, or Passive Battles August 1943–April 1944

MY FIRST LABOR ASSIGNMENT WAS TO THE LARGE SURFACE mine. We lined up in camp, counted off, then marched through a residential part of town to get to the mine. We were no attraction as we marched, since the residents of the town were used to the British POWs already there going to and from work each day. When we arrived at the mine, we saw a large building they used for a warehouse, with a portion where we would eat our noon meal and take a break. We lined up again, counted off, and it was back to work.

What a difference from Tanagawa. Down there, they loaded our cars. We just pushed them out on the bay and dumped them. No stopping. It was round and around, all day. At Aomi, we pushed our car up the hill to where we loaded the ore, loaded it, rode the car down the hill to the scale, had it weighed, pushed it on down to the crusher, and put the trip bar in place. Finally, we dumped the load. Then we went onto another track, and back up the hill. At least the work varied a little.

It also allowed a lot of time for Americans to stand around and talk while we were up there loading cars, continuing our war effort of resistance. The Japanese had set a high quota of cars per day, and the British guys were making that quota, only they were dying because of it. It was different with Americans—maybe it was a pride thing. We had to be motivated to work, and we were not!

We had assessed our options, and one was to hamper the Japanese war effort by dragging what we had—our feet—so that production slowed down. We heard a lot of threats, but there were a lot more Americans than there were Japanese, so they could not beat all of us all the time.

In our first day or so at Aomi, we had been given questionnaires to fill out. We were also given a card to write home. This was repeated each *yasume* day. We were told in military training to only give our captors our names, ranks, and serial numbers. However, in real POW life, things were different. We could answer questions from the Japanese or get beat up. Those camp guards could never check our answers, so I assessed my options and answered the questions.

Most of the questions were about our civilian occupations, schooling, etc. Whatever job a man chose to apply for, he answered the questions accordingly. If a POW really wanted a certain job, he wrote that he had a lot of experience at it. The Japanese could not check, and we took our chances.

What intrigued me was the number of questions concerning tuberculosis. On every questionnaire, the same questions concerning its history in your family appeared. I learned later that the British Army soldiers occupying those countries the Japanese took control of on the Pacific

Rim really had a problem with TB. That may have been one reason they were dying off as POWs. Of course, the questions may have only had something to do with the superstitions of the Japanese. I'm not sure.

We had arrived at Aomi late in the summer—August or September, I believe. It was not bad working the mine in that season. We had plenty of mountain river water to wash up in, and it was sure good to be clean. In fact, we were allowed to swim, too, if we were willing to skinny dip. We swam less and less as the leaves began to turn yellow and red, and autumn began to nip the air.

The corporation we worked for, Mitsui, operated the mine, crusher, a short railroad to the smelter, and owned on out to the main rail line that was the transportation system of Japan—end to end. We went around and around until November. November was the beginning, both years I was there, of the regular rain and snow season. When the rains came, the hill began to slide down. We had to close the mine down for the winter.

My next job was on the smelter. That first morning work detail was unusual indeed. Until that day, I hadn't realized that one of my best army buddies ever had also arrived at Aomi. He was one of the guys from our old Special Duty days on Corregidor whom I had not seen in a long while—a buddy I had not yet located among those 600 POWs.

That morning, we lined up in the main yard in front of our barracks. We counted off, turned right, and were ready to march out when we all could hear a human making the sound of a motorcycle in the crowd. I knew it was my buddy, Joe, acting like he was cranking up his Harley Hog. Boy, how Joe loved his Harley, and he played like he was riding it everywhere he went. He had cranked her up pretty often back on Corregidor, but I'd thought I'd never hear that sound again. Only here was Joe. His motor roared out no different that morning in Aomi, Japan, than it ever had on Corregidor. I'd have recognized that engine anywhere.

I knew he was in our group that day, but before I could find him, we had to go to the smelter. I had to work my shift, then hope to meet him again after we returned to our barracks. When word of mouth is all you have, 600 men is a lot of men to search through in a POW camp. I finally did manage to find Joe.

He clasped my shoulders and I clasped his. "Man, you been on a diet?" he asked.

I cuffed him and replied, "Listen, Mr. Bones, fatten up before you have a whole lot to say." We didn't get to hear what had happened since Corregidor for each of us, or reminisce, because POWs weren't allowed to talk to each other unless the guards couldn't see you. At any rate, it was good to know Joe was still alive.

Back to my new job—once we arrived at the smelter, most of the other guys were regulars on that detail. They knew what their jobs were, so they began their regular work schedule. But new guys had to be taught. The first assignment for me was that they strapped a wooden box to my back; shades of the big Korean. The straps went over my shoulders, under my arms, and around my waist. The bottom of the box was hinged, with a plaited grass rope over my shoulder to hold it closed.

I sat on a stool and let someone load my box while I held the tail rope tight. I carried the thing across the floor of the smelter, climbed metal stairs, turned my back to a huge melting pot, and dumped my box of ore. Then I walked back over the same patch for another load. It was another one of those around and around jobs that seemed to have no end.

This old boy failed to see the need to hurry. Besides, that grass rope was hurting my shoulder. I assessed my options and just had to dump a few loads on the smelter floor. Those guards were not happy at all. I got very little sympathy and a bunch of knots on my head. The guards knocked me down and kicked me, trying to make their point. It was a bad first day on the job. In fact, I had more trouble learning that job than any I can remember. I was not cut out to carry one of those boxes of ore. I had bad day after bad day on that smelter job. I had to think of something, because those knots on my head were beginning to hurt.

Three Anglos made life a lot better for all of us at Aomi: two American doctors and an English chaplain. One doctor, I'll name him Dr. Do Good, was a regular American Army doctor, and he had the solution to my smelter problem. The other, whom I shall call Dr. Cut Up, was an elderly Navy doctor. He had a set of scalpels he loved to play with as he listened to your story, and he always wanted to operate on someone. The English chaplain, whom I shall call Preacher, was a jewel of a fellow. He was also a radioman, and knew how to persuade the Japanese concerning things to make life better. He loved the Lord and served Him well in that camp.

Back at the smelter job, the next *yasume* day came. I wrote my card to my mother, and then picked up the questionnaire. Those questions popped up concerning tuberculosis. Rumor was going around that the camp had what was called the "Garden Party" for sick guys. My inner voice shouted, *Why not apply*? I wrote that I didn't know about myself, but everyone in my family I could think of had some kind of tuberculosis.

I was not the only one who applied. Several others had decided to take their chances. After all, it was winter in northern Japan. Sure enough, we were summoned to sick call. We had learned early how to run a fever by placing a sliver of soap under our tongues. The old mercury thermometers would register a fever when you did that. With a friendly doctor in Dr. Do Good, we had it made.

The sole purpose of the Garden Party was to keep those who may have had tuberculosis away from the Japanese. That turned out to be a pretty good winter detail. It was too cold to have a garden, so we had to clean up around the camp. All we had to do was police the area and avoid coming near the Japanese.

This old country boy managed to stay out of trouble for a while. It was not long before we had the camp in pretty good shape. There was no place to put the snow, so it stacked up to eight or ten feet deep in the yard. It was too heavy for us to shovel, so the men just walked on it, even in formations. The Japanese were forced to think of something else for the garden party to do.

There was a huge rock warehouse down the street from camp, cold but dry inside. The Japanese didn't store much there, because war material had become scarce. Food supplies were low, too. Our rations had been cut again, probably to about 375 calories, which was the lowest they ever gave us. We were taken over and left to clean up the old warehouse. At least we did not have to deal with the guards each day. We just wandered around the warehouse to see what we could find. Cold, but dry without head knocking, became a good thing.

Toward the back of the warehouse, I found a shelf of bright red parachutes. I thought red would be easy to spot as a paratrooper sailed toward the ground—kind of a stupid choice of color for a parachute. Maybe that made the Japanese military think them defective. Maybe since that red circle was the center of Japan's flag, they simply hadn't used them yet. On the other hand, maybe they were civilian pleasure-jumpers' equipment. It made no difference—there they were, all wrapped in nice coverings, just waiting for me. The summer before, up at the mine, I had been wondering if I couldn't figure out something to wear next summer when it was time to jump into that river of clear, cold mountain spring water once again. The parachutes offered me the perfect solution.

"Hey, any of you guys help me find some shears?" I called to the rest.

The scissors were quickly located, and while the others stood around laughing, I opened one pack and carefully cut enough of that beautiful red silk material to make swimming trunks. I also snitched enough of that white cord to trim them with. "Anybody else need some new swimming attire?" I asked, before I carefully replaced the covering and hid the material under my clothing. Nobody else in the Garden Party felt the need to have any of that material. I think they probably wondered what would happen if mine were discovered. One thing I know—if the Japanese ever used those parachutes, someone had a big surprise.

Back in camp, I hid my loot in my bedroll until the next *yasume* day. We were permitted to check out sewing kits to repair our clothing. I checked one out and brought it back to my bunk. POWs gathered around as I held the material up to my bony hips, measured, and modeled. They chuckled quietly and slapped me on the back.

Kirby—a buddy I'd worked with at the mine now and then—said, "Baker, you've got the guts of an army mule."

I cut thirty-inch waist swimming trunks, sewed them up, sewed on the trim, and stowed it for hot weather. Mom would have been proud—my stitches were nice and even, if somewhat long.

Guess what? When summer *did* come, I was afraid to wear it. I realized, perhaps a little late, that those Japanese guards would have gone totally nuts if I'd shown up in red trunks.

However, I did manage to hang on to it and bring it home with me. It still reminds me of how slim I was. Six feet tall, and I only weighed about 100 pounds. At least I suppose I had about 100 pounds of skin and bones. There certainly wasn't much muscle left, and I never got much thinner or lost much more weight.

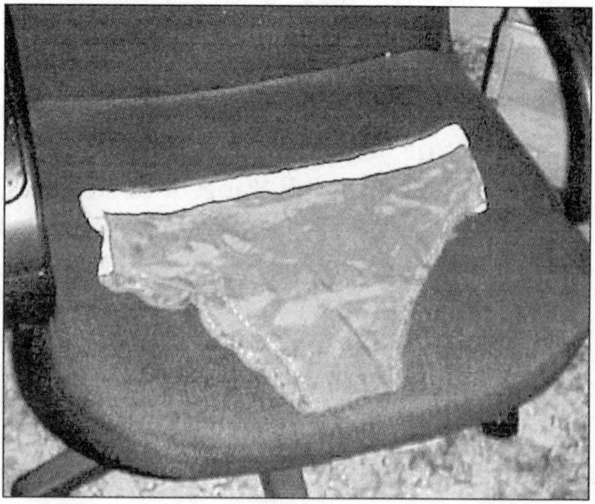

It was not long until spring came. The sun came out, the snow melted, and the Garden Party was taken into a field to plant a garden.

We were enjoying the sunshine when, at sick call one morning, Dr. Do Good said, "The Japanese are talking about sending those who might have tuberculosis to Tokyo for treatment, or *whatever*." Only a few days later, my fever subsided. I was pronounced fit for a work detail by Dr. Do Good, and I was relieved of my Garden Party duty.

The snow had melted from the hillside, the ground was about dry, and the mine was ready to reopen. *What a nice place to enjoy the summer*, I was thinking. Sure enough, I got the detail again.

Before we open that mine, let me tell you something funny I heard happened to my friend, Joe. His motorcycle riding seemed to be driving those Japanese guards up the wall. The camp commander apparently made a plan to deal with Joe's motorcycle.

The guards called Joe out one *yasume* day. They allowed him to ride his motorcycle over to see the camp commander in the headquarters building. Later, we heard that Joe stood before that colonel, with a guard on either side. The colonel carefully and quietly explained to Joe why he could not keep his motorcycle in camp. Then the commander told the guards to take the motorcycle over to the other side of the room and destroy it. The guards pretended to take the motorcycle and beat it to total destruction with their rifle butts. The colonel then explained to Joe why his Harley Hog would not run. He told Joe to return to his barracks and enjoy his *yasume* day.

Joe promptly saluted the colonel, pretended to crank up his Harley, and rode on out of the office. That was the last time those guards complained. They just let Joe ride on. I sure do wish I had seen all that for myself.

What I Didn't Know—3

(US fortunes of war, August 1943–April 1944)

On August 14, 1943, Prime Minister Churchill and his chiefs of staff, and President Roosevelt, along with his chiefs of staff, were meeting at the Quadrant Conference in the United States. To coordinate the Allies' strategies took many conferences of this sort. The Quadrant Conference developed a plan for the invasion of France, and an agreement to share with Great Britain the scientific information on the atomic bomb being developed in Los Alamos, New Mexico. Little did I know that, not far from my hometown, the tools of the greatest destruction man has ever known were in the works.

I also didn't know a little girl from Nagasaki—living her life like any seven-year-old, going to school, learning from her parents.

On August 17, General MacArthur—chomping at the bit to return to the Philippines—caught the Japanese air base at Wewak in New Guinea on the ground, and destroyed it. He said, "Nothing is so helpless as an airplane on the ground," probably recalling the first day of the Philippine invasion.

The Pacific War of 1943/44 saw us take places with unfamiliar names—places like Lae, Salamua, Bougainville, and Rabaul—over the next months. We fought on the ground, in the sky, and at sea. The Atoll War cost us many brave men in these months of the war, also. The Japanese had begun to run in the Pacific. Americans were clamoring for more support for the Pacific War—so much so that Prime Minister Churchill was concerned that President Roosevelt would not give England, who was running out of resources, the power needed to continue the war in Europe and Africa. And then something happened that changed life considerably for Pacific POWs and the people of Japan.

In Los Alamos, New Mexico, the best of the American scientists, and some Jewish ones who'd escaped Germany, had been developing the atomic bomb. "Little Boy," for Hiroshima, and "Fat Man," for Nagasaki, were just about ready.

The Amazing Men of Aomi
April–November 1944

MEANWHILE, BACK AT THE MINE OPENING, WE LINED UP, counted off, and marched down the residential street to the mine. What a difference! We found the Japanese had hired more supervisors. They were planning to increase our production this year. Working harder, eating less—interesting concept.

Kirby had become my new car partner. We were told we had to produce ten cars per day, so we hopped right to, pushing our car up to the place of loading.

"Here's my three stones," Kirby said.

"OK, here's mine," I answered.

We threw the stones into the car, and down to the crusher we went, in record time.

The supervisors did not like that. We were chewed out royally and sent up to get a whole load. I figured if we had to do this stupid work, at least we could have a little fun at it, but I held my laughter tight all the way back, as we pushed the car up the mountain.

This time, I said, "Kirb, the art of car filling deserves our best resources." We filled the car with as much wet dirt as possible, put a row of stones around the edge, filled that with loose dirt, then stacked up another row of stones.

Kirby gave the car a little shove to check the weight, and said, "I believe we ought to get double pay for this. We've got at least two carloads on this car."

When they started us down, the weight of our car spread the light tracks and down the car went into the dirt between the tracks. This time, the whole crew were holding their sides, trying not to laugh out loud. After the supervisors beat the sap out of us, the Japanese worked for most of the morning trying to get the car to the crusher and the tracks back where they were supposed to go. We got knocked around a little more, and were told to try again. Mitsui faced a no-win situation trying to get decent work out of American POWs.

One vicious Japanese civilian worker on mine detail would try to kill POWs for fun. We had to watch him, know exactly where he was, continually. He used a jack-hammer, set explosives, and blew the side of the mountain down so we could haul it to the crusher. While we worked, he sat on the rocks waiting to be needed again, and he wore a big piece of tanned dog skin sewed to the seat of his pants. I guess it cushioned his seat. We nicknamed him Rabbit Ass. He actually liked being called that, but that nickname helped catch him after the war. They considered him a Class C war criminal.

Rabbit Ass would climb around the mountainside, pry a large boulder loose, let it roll down almost to his intended victim, then he'd yell. He'd laugh like crazy when the POW he'd marked for crushing began scrambling to get out of the way of the boulder. Sometimes his victim made it out of the way, and sometimes he didn't. Rabbit Ass' insanity was a pain in the neck, day after day, all summer long.

One day, Kirby and I were loading, and that insane yell came right above us.

"Run!" we yelled simultaneously, not even knowing which direction to head. The boulder rumbled over a cliff and landed on our car before bouncing on down the mountain. "Asshole!" Kirby hissed, and flipped the finger in Rabbit Ass' direction, as laughter rang out over the mountain.

We went back to loading our car, and I'll be darned if it wasn't less than a quarter of an hour when the yell came again. We took to our heels. This time, the boulder was a little to the left of where the first one had been, and if I'd been a foot in front of where I was, they could have slipped me under the door when we got back to the barracks.

"If there's any justice in Hell," I said, as we got back to our car, "Rabbit Ass will be rolled under boulders all day long, forever."

On the other hand, we had a couple of real blessings that summer. One of our guys was a chiropractor. Most states did not recognize them as real doctors, so Johnnie, as I've named him, was just one of us boys. Nevertheless, when a back went out, that Johnny knew how to fix it up, and he enjoyed doing it, too. We'd go into his barracks, nod, point to the pain, lay down on the shelf, and away he'd go, pulling and prodding. He never missed.

However, Johnnie had a big problem. He had let the Japanese literally drive him nuts. He had certain things he did, and he would knock out a Japanese guard who tried to stop him. He didn't talk, either. He didn't talk to the POWs—except maybe "Where's it hurt?"—and he absolutely didn't talk to the Japanese. One of his habits was to wear two full canteens of water on his Army equipment belt. Not one, but two—always. Perhaps that's not extremely odd, but it became a problem for Johnnie.

One evening we were in camp, washing up at our line of sinks in the hallway, when Johnnie—wearing his canteen belt with two canteens of water on it—had a run-in with a guard. The guard yelled something nobody understood. He grabbed Johnnie by the shoulders and started to reach to unbuckle his canteen belt.

As usual, Johnnie didn't talk. Before we knew what happened, he took off one Army green canteen of water. I wondered for a second if he was going to give it to the guard. Instead, he knocked the guard over the head with it, and the next thing that guard knew, he was listening to the birdies sing. That's all Johnnie did. He didn't look at us when it was over. He didn't say anything. He returned to washing. Two other guards came and carried off the guard he'd downed. After that, most of them stayed clear of Johnnie.

In June 1944, the rumor mill told us that the US had begun to bomb the main island of Japan—mostly daylight runs. That put a whole new dimension on our war experience, a long-awaited one. The Japanese thought their antiaircraft guns would shoot the B-29s down, but we told them, "No way. They will just keep coming!" And they did. Thank God, they did.

The night of one *yasume* day, about eleven-thirty or midnight, our British Army chaplain—the one we called Preacher—came into our barracks. "Boys," he said, "I must speak quietly, and I cannot take questions. I have a radio operating in the upper beams of my barrack. It receives American newscasts. I will listen from time to time, and tell you men the news from home.

"However, to protect this operation, I have persuaded the Japanese colonel to allow an American to guard the perimeter of the barracks at night. I explained to him that we might have a fire, and we did not want to request more Japanese guards. Will you serve a couple of hours of guard duty?"

Would we? To really know how our guys were faring in the war, we'd have let him have our soap. So, for us, it was on guard for two hours, then wake the next guy on the list. We began to know more about how the war was going than our guards did. My hope transplant was getting major reinforcement.

Through all this, the mine detail kept right on working. Every day we had our usual knocking around. Most of us figured we might as well earn it, so we bedeviled those Japanese as much as possible. Anything was better than work that helped them with their war effort. Hard work was the reason the English Army POWs died off, so we also learned a lesson from them and avoided work at all costs.

Now, not only did that preacher listen to the radio, he loved to talk about Jesus. So, he persuaded the Japanese to let him have a service in the recreation hall every *yasume* day. They put one requirement on his preaching: he could say nothing about God. All the floors were wooden, so he stood at the head of the recreation hall, with the hallway running behind him.

"Boys, we're slaves, and the Japanese can starve us, beat us, give us little or no medical attention, and everything else they do, but God has not forgotten us. He's here and He cares. I believe, and I know it to be true, that He is here in Aomi, walking with each one of you in whatever you face. He's here when they beat you; He's here when Rabbit Ass shoves boulders down at you. He's here when they hand you bugged rice. He loves you, and..." The footfalls of Japanese army boots could be heard on the hallway floor. "The best thing for us to do in our situation is to work obediently. We will avoid getting into trouble, and perhaps the guards will even increase our rations. I hope you are all writing your letters home. It means a lot to our loved ones to know that we are well." The sound of the boots went out of earshot down the hallway. "And Jesus went through the kind of things we are going through. He understands us. Do you know He even said that if we hang on, we'll come out of this stronger and better men than we went in? Maybe not physically, but on the inside, where it matters." Only God could have given the preacher the ability to stand in the face of the enemy in all the ways he did.

As the summer of 1944 wore on, things began to get worse. There was more knocking around, trying to get more and more work out of us. Nevertheless, someone came upon another way to frustrate the Japanese guards. If a POW believed he could whip a Japanese guard he didn't like, all he had to do was tell another guard the guy would not wrestle him. Those people loved their wrestling matches, so they would berate the victim until he agreed to wrestle.

They would draw a ring on the ground. Everyone gathered around, and the match began. Anything was fair game, and no one helped either one. They would fight to the cheers of the crowd until one could no longer continue. Only a few Americans took that challenge, and definitely not me. I was busy staying alive.

One way we found to help us stay alive was at this house we passed going to and from the mine. It had a persimmon tree in the front yard. We'd been eying those green persimmons all summer. One afternoon they looked a little bit ripe. As we marched under the tree limbs, one guy and then another reached up, and off came the persimmons. They were eaten by the time we got to camp. We were still eating 375 calories per day then, and an extra persimmon was just another way to keep on keeping on.

Another day at the smelter, Joe had an accident. He mangled his right leg so badly that Dr. Cut Up amputated it above the knee. What a sad way to live as a POW, with only one leg. When his leg went, so did his spirit. The accident even put his Harley Hog out of action. We all missed it.

Then, on a beautiful, clear day in early November, we had finished our lunch break at the mine and were lined up to count off and return to work. My friend, Johnnie, came out in his complete rain gear, canteens and all. He wore a large bamboo Chinese coolie hat on his head, and a woven straw cover over his shoulders. One of our three Japanese guards went totally out of control. He yelled and screamed in Japanese. He told Johnnie to remove his rain gear.

Johnnie replied, "Gonna rain! Gonna rain!" That's all he would say. The guard ran in to pull the gear off, and at that moment, a full canteen landed on his head. The other two guards eased slowly in and pulled the first guard away. They revived him, talked it over, and decided to allow Johnnie to wear the rain gear, even though the sun was shining and it was hot.

About the middle of the afternoon, the clouds came in. It began to rain, and I mean *hard*. Within three hours, we had a flood that would not quit. The whole mountainside began to slide down. All of us—Japanese and POWs—had to run like crazy. We were dodging sliding mud, running over the top of it, staying out of the way of rocks coming down, and trying not to bowl each other over. It would have been a good chance to escape, if there'd been anywhere to go, but our American faces would have stuck out in the Asian crowd like sore thumbs.

How Johnnie knew in advance that the flood was coming, I do not know, but it came. That day became the closing bell for the mine for 1944. All any of us could do was make our way back to the barracks, where we prepared for the winter of 1944 and 1945.

White Christmas
Winter 1944–Spring 1945

THE WINTER OF 1944/45 COULD BE DESCRIBED IN ONE WORD: *snow*. It snowed more than this old country boy had ever seen before or since, which is saying a lot, because snow drifts in the Panhandle can cover the side of a house.

We finally stopped trying to dig out the barracks. The guys from downstairs came upstairs and left through the upstairs windows when they needed to go out. We only kept enough snow off the roof to prevent a cave-in, to avoid being buried alive.

The radio news of the war was good. Our preacher friend was the greatest—he had hooked that radio into the barracks' electric power without the Japanese knowing. He took real chances when he listened, and then went from barracks to barracks spreading the good news. The Philippine campaign was going great. MacArthur had finally come back.

Every *yasume* day, that good man of God would continually tell us the truth of God and how we should believe and trust in Jesus. I don't know what religion he claimed, but I do know God was with that old preacher.

It got to be about Christmastime, still snowing. No doubt about it—we would have a white Christmas. As usual in Japan, there were no gifts, Christmas tree, or singing of Christmas carols. Instead, we kept on playing the waiting game.

On Christmas Day, 1944, a lot of the POWs including me were called out for a work detail to remove snow from warehouse roofs. The guards came in through the window and pointed to the ones they wanted. We were all still wearing only the shirts, pants, and sandals we'd worn since we'd been in Japan; when a guard pointed at me, I hoped what they wanted us for wasn't outside. Then one of them opened the window again, and the barracks went silent. They began marching us out the window.

One of those chosen with me whispered, as we marched out through the open window, "You s'pose this means we're getting warm clothes and boots?" Another snickered, and got a rifle butt in the ribs.

The cold hit me before I even reached the open window, its razor blast tearing through my worn shirt. I looked about for a way to disappear from this line of skeletons heading into the ice house, but there were too many guards watching. As I stepped over the windowsill, the wind hit me full force. I stumbled, receiving, as the other man had, a rifle butt reminder—mine to get myself back into motion. As the falling snow hit me, it melted, and I began to shiver.

By the time we marched to the area where we were to work, I had already begun to stiffen from the cold. They gave us each a shovel and assigned me to a warehouse roof with a few other men. No time went by before I realized my feet were going numb. The falling snow had stopped melting and begun sticking to my shoulders and my eyelashes. Loosening the snow on the roof was nearly impossible because it had frozen solid. The guards went inside the warehouse. I assumed they were gathered around some kind of heat, but watching out the windows.

I called out, "Any of you guys having any luck with this stuff?"

"No," one dared to reply.

I'm not sure whether assessing my options and using what I had worked out for better or worse under these circumstances. I thought about escaping from the roof, but it was a sure bet I'd just get lost in the blizzard and freeze to death before anyone found me. Instead, I dug a six-foot hole in the snow on that warehouse roof. In there, at least I could stay out of the wind. Nevertheless, standing there in the snow all day with no winter clothes or shoes, after the numbness, my feet and legs began to burn while the rest of me shook with cold.

My breath made mist, and for a while I amused myself with smoke rings, but trying to keep a positive attitude slowly became merely trying not to freeze solid. I poked at the snow around me, just to keep moving, because I knew I'd freeze to death if I ever crouched down looking for a little more warmth the way my body ached for me to do. Besides, maybe the guards were listening for the sound of shoveling.

No one brought lunch that day—nothing broke up the white death, until at last the guards came out to take us back to the barracks before night fell. My face was stiff and covered with snow, and I could hardly see. I managed to climb out of my hole anyway. I picked up each wooden leg and made it follow the other, the guards shoving me and the others, now and then trying to get a little speed out of us. No other POW was in any better shape. The march back could hardly have been called a march—more like a funeral procession—and it took far longer to return than the same trip had taken in the morning.

When we at last arrived in the barracks, the others pulled off our frozen clothes and arranged us as close to the hibachis as we could be put. It took hours for me to stop shaking. Finally, when my clothes were dry again, and we all were in a little better shape, we were treated to a Christmas present. Two men split a standard Red Cross package weighing about eleven or twelve pounds.

"Oh man! Look, soap, shaving gear, and cigarettes!" Kirby cried. "We can use 'em or we can sell 'em."

We could sell soap and cigarettes for paper money that the US treasury wrote off in 1941 in Manila that seemed to spring up in Japan in 1945. The money was very useful in northern Japan, because the Japanese didn't know it wasn't any good in the United States. They traded Japanese yen for those dollars each time they had the opportunity. There was also a black market going on among POWs. Some of those guys just had to smoke, so if you decided not to smoke, your cigs were worth a lot of money.

What we all liked best was the food. There were salmon, raisins, powdered milk, instant coffee, even a can of peach jam. It was a delicious feast to a bunch of men who had been living on 350 calories of rice per day for what seemed like forever.

We had the finish of a pretty nice Christmas. That night, however, the men of my barracks realized that my legs had frozen, and I was in sorry shape. Both legs burned like fire as they thawed out, and were so tender I couldn't walk.

"Listen, Bake," Kirby said, "I know this is crap, but I think you better let Doc Cut Up amputate them. I saw another guy get gangrene before I came to Aomi, and a POW without legs isn't pretty, but gangrene will kill you."

"No."

"I don't want to watch you die, soldier," Kirby persisted.

"Listen, Kirby. If you were those Japanese, and your job was to dig a mine with a bunch of slave POWs, would you feed one with no legs?"

He hung his head, "I guess not," he answered.

"I'm going home pretty soon. We'll work the legs out then. But in the meantime, I'm walking on them."

February, March, and April of 1945 brought real good news to a lot of hurting POWs, and I mean hurting. My thawed legs never stopped aching as if pricked by a million needles—not one day, not one minute. I became a master at ignoring pain.

However, the Philippine campaign was being completed, and B29s added night raids to their day raids on Tokyo and other places in Japan. This was another boost to my hope transplant. It made me feel like I could do anything just to hold on long enough to see Texas and my mother again. The Japanese at Aomi knew nothing of the war, and once spring arrived, they insisted we go back and open the mine. My legs had recovered enough by then for me to work.

That's when Kirby and I decided to shut the mine down.

These Bombers Are Ours!
Summer 1945

After the Japanese gave up on getting the car we'd ridden down the mountainside out of the crusher, they decided Kirby and I should be punished. Their anger had not played out, and they needed to vent. That evening, we were taken to the front of the camp guardhouse, where we were made to kneel down. Just as had happened in the Philippines at Cabanatuan, we were each given a stick to hold over our heads.

I wondered whether I had enough strength left to do this again. However, I knew to expect the numbness, and once it kicked in, all I had to do was stay awake. Sometime during the night, they pushed us off the stools, and we returned to the barracks.

The chill before sunrise found me struggling to get out from under my blanket. I imagine Kirby had the same problem. I could feel every bone in my body—every one ached. Nevertheless, I tried to look at things positively. For instance, every time I moved, some of my bones seemed to get back into place. The pain continued, though.

Kirby and I were lucky, I suppose. Neither of us was killed. Maybe we were still alive because these guards worked for Mitsui, not the Japanese Army. They had a bottom line to think about, so they weren't as committed to our destruction. Then again, maybe we all were growing tired of war.

The weather had warmed a little by the time we ate our meager rice ration and got out into the yard. When Kirby and I met in the yard, he asked, "You hurt?"

"Only from my neck down," I answered. With those guards around, we could not discuss our plight openly. So we silently expressed our mutual sympathy.

The Japanese still had a shut-down mine and a lot of idle workers, though. That day, everyone in camp dealt with confusion. The work detail sat around waiting for instructions, but that only gave Kirby and me another opportunity to nurse our wounds. After I cleaned the blood off myself, I wrapped my blanket around my back to see if I could warm it up a little. We saw high-level discussions going on between the camp commander and the guards, but nothing came of them. Confusion ruled the day.

However, we did not have to wait long for something to happen. I don't know the exact date, but Navy dive-bombers paid a visit to the smelter, as well as to the branch railroad track to the main rail line. As I watched, my mind went back to Monkey Point, and I thought, *this one's for you, Red. That's one for you, Sergeant Brady*, as the bombs fell. A sense of satisfaction came over me, and judging from the faces of the other POWs, they felt it, too. The bombers shut down the whole mining and smelting operation for as long as I knew about.

I guess during that run, the bombers had noticed our camp, because soon one of those gorgeous silver planes flew in very low and dropped a note in the compound which read, "It will not be very long before you have help." That note was passed around the POWs until it was a tattered scrap. I personally was not about to give up, but I wonder how many others were saved from tossing in the towel because of that note.

The next day, several planes came back to the camp. Some dove in close and dropped boxed food and supplies, while the others watched overhead. That was like Christmas in July. The boxes were broken up in the fall, but we all scrambled about, picking up the parcels. That American food went through our kitchen in a hurry. The smell of the meat cooking was enough to bring tears to our eyes. Add that to the vegetables and bread, and it sure tasted good to a bunch of slave-labor POWs.

In the midst of all that, I could understand what the Japanese supervisors and the mine owner were thinking. They had the same question all other corporation people have: *what will our bottom line look like with this mine shut down?*

If they put in play what I used—assess your options and use what you have—what situation were they in? They had 600 potential slave laborers in camp with nothing to do, although they still had to be fed those 350 calories of rice every day. That is 210,000 calories of rice, each day, being eaten without any productivity at all. I think what each man weighed at that point was the weight of his skin and bones. Mine weigh ninety-eight pounds, which I was to find out in August. We were barely hanging on. In addition to approximately 600 workers sitting idle in camp, there was a mine shut down and a broken down, bombed-out smelter.

On the other hand, there was an amount of raw ore in the plant yard, and a few molded ingots ready to ship. Their solution became to put us to work fixing the railroad. If that branch line were fixed, the ore and ingots could be shipped, with the money going to their bottom line. We became a railroad maintenance gang for the time being.

It proved a large task to convince 600 slaves, who were expecting to be released any day, to see the point of fixing that railroad. We used various means to stall, day in and day out. The supervisors were Japanese civilians who were as hungry as we were. I guess their compassion for us allowed them to help us, by standing around talking with us rather than forcing living skeletons to work hard.

Nevertheless, we eventually put the side track in usable condition, except for one little switch where the tram road joined the main line. One POW was "foolish" enough to place a rock in the switch, holding it open enough to derail the lead car.

As we watched the cars steam off into the dirt, one of the guys said, "Well, son of a gun! Will you look at that?" under his breath. He spoke for all of us. Passive resistance was alive and well among us. The other cars never made it onto the main rail line, and the corporation bottom line again headed for trouble. We'd found another way to hinder the Japanese war effort.

After that, we all hung around camp listening as much as possible to Preacher's updates on our radio news, which was encouraging. The war had ended in Europe. MacArthur was back in the Philippines. The preacher said that, aided by the British, American B-29s were bombing the Japanese main island on a regular basis. We knew it was a matter of time before the war would come to an end for the rest of us, but those Japanese guards still found excuses to knock us around. They couldn't hear our radio.

On August 6, 1945, Preacher came through the barracks whispering. He said, "The news is that the United States has dropped the first atomic bomb ever made by man on Hiroshima, in the southern part of the main island."

Camp Aomi wasn't close enough for us to see any sign of it. The radio said the concussion flattened everything for miles. My mind couldn't imagine the devastation it must have caused. Nevertheless, the Japanese gave no sign of surrender in our camp, and the radio indicated no sign of their accepting defeat in any of the last outposts in the South Pacific.

On August 9, 1945, Preacher came through again. "The United States dropped the second atomic bomb on Nagasaki, also in the southern part of Japan," he told us. The news still gave no word that Japan would surrender, even though two large industrial cities had been laid waste by one single bomb each.

Following those broadcasts, we learned that about 800 B-29 bombers raided the Tokyo area on August 14, 1945. This was one of the most devastating raids of the war. The same day, they reported that about 140 B29 bombers raided the Akita petroleum import refining and distribution center for all of Japan, about 270 miles northwest of Tokyo.

I learned later that the hardliners in Tokyo were still holding out for the idea of fighting to the last Japanese after an American invasion. I didn't hear the statement Emperor Hirohito issued to his warlords, because I was outside the barracks, walking back and forth on fire watch.

Preacher heard it, and came down and told me what the emperor said.

> "I cannot bear to see my innocent people suffer any longer. It pains me to think of those who served me so faithfully. The soldiers and sailors who have been killed or wounded in far-off battles. The families who have lost all their worldly goods, and often their lives.
>
> "The time has come when we must bear the unbearable. I swallow my tears and give my sanction to the proposal to accept the Allied proclamation."

With that statement, our surrender proclamation was accepted.

Clapping me on the shoulder, Preacher said, "Well, the war is finally over. The American and British fleets are off the coast of Japan and ready to come and get us."

I felt renewed strength—energy I hadn't felt in four years. "Let's wake the fellows and celebrate!" I yelled. "It's over!" He nodded me close to his ear and said, "Hold on, soldier. Those Japanese guards do not know the war is over yet. They have the guns. Half the men would be killed or wounded if we tell them before the Japanese know."

We waited for the guards to learn the news in their official way.

War No More—A POW Slave Goes Free August 1945

I JOINED SICK CALL THE NEXT MORNING, RUNNING A LITTLE "soap fever." I wanted Dr. Do Good to provide my exemption from any work detail, because I expected the Japanese to find out the war was over and I wanted to be in camp for it. However, it turned out to be the longest day of my life—absolutely no word about the war from anyone. I had lain on my mat all night knowing the war was finally over, but also knowing those Japanese in charge had no idea of our good news, and I had to keep quiet. The waiting had never been this hard.

The next morning broke the same. Work details reported and marched off as usual. The Japanese guards and camp commander went about their normal business. Those few POWs in camp trudged through another in a long string of mindless days. Only two POWs—Preacher and I—knew the good news, which must remain secret for the safety of the men. The wait for the Japanese commander to learn that news was interminable for me. I'm sure it was no easier for our fine preacher man.

Finally, about noon on August 15, 1945, all the work details shuffled into camp early. As usual, none of them knew what was happening. They were following orders. When everyone was told to remain in the compound area, I began to suspect that the Japanese had finally learned of their surrender. All POWs were ordered to stay in their groups. Those POWs left in the barracks were called into the compound.

A few of the guards carried out the small stand our Japanese commander used to make his official speeches and set it before us. In a moment, he walked from his headquarters, as straight-shouldered as ever, head up. He mounted the stand, and looked about for quiet.

"Thank you," he said in English, "for your good conduct in camp. The war is over. The Japanese have surrendered." He looked down at his boots for a second, then up again at us. "I wish everyone the best of luck with your loved ones back home. You are dismissed." He stepped down from the stand, and it was taken behind him to his headquarters.

All this was over, in five sentences. I don't know what I expected, but I was floored. I wouldn't have been any more astonished if he'd gotten up there and said, "The end."

In the ranks of the POWs, rejoicing commenced—dancing and waving of arms in the air, laughing and shouting, knocking each other around. I think I heard snatches of *God Bless America* and the *Star Spangled Banner* being sung. Yet, at the same time, confusion reigned. After the initial elation, the POWs realized that no information at all was available about what we were to do now. Moments ago, we were told when to do everything from eating to bathing. Were we now each the captain of our ship? Who would take command? The preacher man tried to calm the men down, but it was talk, talk, and talk. Each man seemed to have his own idea about how to accept freedom.

"Thirty-nine months being told what to do in this damn Japanese camp is over!" one soldier yelled.

Another asked, "What do we do now?"

And another, "Are we free?"

The general cry was, "*What should we do?*"

I couldn't even decide what I was free from. If I were to find freedom in the immediate future, where would it be? I could do whatever I wanted, but I had been ordered about so long I didn't even know what I wanted.

We saw the Japanese commander leave the camp with his entourage, and all the Japanese guards soon followed. That pointed out our problem, even to those who were still celebrating. Who would organize 600 men, becoming our leader for the near future? Six hundred starving men with a sudden gift of freedom could present a major problem.

As we had so many times in the past, we assessed our options and used what we had. We decided the first option we'd exercise was to eat lunch. Those who stayed in camp on any other day had forfeited lunch, because lunch was eaten on work details. Since we could—and perhaps because it had previously been forbidden—some of the guys began rummaging around the guardhouse, trying to find food. Others just lay around, assuming, I guess, that rescue would come right away and they'd had enough of work—even rummaging for food.

Kirby and an Irishman I'll call O'Brien, as well as myself, had found each other.

"Let's mosey into town and see what it's like there," I

suggested. I was tired of buggy rice, and I figured even if the guys rummaging for food came up with any, lunch would only be more of the same.

Lacking a better plan, Kirby and O'Brien agreed. Off we walked, I think all of us half-expecting someone to stop us. We walked right through those gates—no guns in our faces, no beatings. Freedom. As we passed one house after another, it amazed me how friendly the Japanese civilians were. They felt as glad as we did that the war was over.

Before long, we came to a house with an old-fashioned wooden barber pole painted red and white. "I've got some funny money. Let's have a shave and a haircut," Kirby said, heading inside.

"Might as well," O'Brien agreed. "We've seen about everything there is to see in this town. What's one more Japanese with a straight razor to my throat?"

I followed them inside, wondering what in the world this barber was going to cut off me. I had no hair on my face, and very little left on my head.

The Japanese barber was a nice fellow who had his shop in his home. We knew enough Japanese by this time to talk a while. Like us, he was glad the war was over, and he was hoping to receive soap and cigarettes from the States again. I guess, after all, it *is* the little things in life. He told us that he and his wife had a goose hidden under their house. They kept it for an egg once in a while. He also said that if they could procure some rice, she would kill the goose, bake it with the fixings, and we could all have dinner with them the next night.

"Let's go down to the rice warehouse by the railroad tracks," Kirby said. "I'll bet nobody's watching it."

"The man here has a bicycle, for sure," O'Brien said hopefully.

Off we went, pushing the bike down to the warehouse, since we couldn't all ride it. Sure enough, no one was around, so we pried open the door, slapped a sixty-pound sack of rice on the bike's seat, and walked it back to the barber's house. We met the barber's wife, spent the rest of the afternoon enjoying our freedom, and then returned to camp, having made friends with folks who'd been the enemy just days before.

Back in camp, those Britishers were all out in the compound. The ranking men in camp had taken charge. They were practicing their drills so they could present themselves, in a manner that would be pleasing to the Queen, to whomsoever came to rescue them. They kept this up all our daylight hours.

As far as Kirby, O'Brien, and I were concerned, our best option was going to that Japanese home for dinner the next evening. We each used what we had—two feet to walk on, and an empty stomach to fill.

I am happy to report that our goose-and-rice dinner was a complete success. The aroma of that goose stew had our mouths watering clear down the street before we even arrived at the house. I ate as much as my shrunken stomach would hold. That home-cooked food was the best ever to hungry POWs and a family glad the war was over.

We left stuffed and returned to camp, where the Americans were considerably different than the British. The only officers we had in camp were those two doctors, and they were not going to take charge of anything. They were ready to go home. We were all hanging around, waiting for whatever information we could get, which was mostly from the preacher's radio. He kept listening, then he'd report to the camp any news concerning when we could expect help. This went on for a few days.

He reported that an American aerial mapping squadron was mapping the area around Tokyo and Yokohama, so that an occupation force could be landed. The British and American occupying forces could then begin evacuation of POWs—but, of course, the logistics would take time.

There were still pockets of resistance to anything American. Our rescue was a matter of preparing the landing. Our troops would also have to make sure things were taken care of in an orderly fashion. The precious time this required felt like eternity to us.

Kirby drummed his fingers on a table and spoke for us all. "When I was a slave, one more hour, one more day, one more week made no difference. Now that I'm free, I want out of here, and I mean now!"

On the other hand, it wasn't long before the Air Force began to drop fifty-five–gallon drums of food and supplies to all known POW camps. However, ours did not always land in the camp compound. Japanese civilians were hungry, too. It became sort of a dogfight as to who got to the barrel of food first. The barrels usually broke open in the fall, and for us, it was grab food and run.

Most days, the British contingent of Camp Aomi was quite busy. The Britishers were still trying to prepare to look good for the Queen, but she was halfway around the world. Maybe it was some young officer trying to score a brownie point or two toward a promotion. Oh well—it's anyone's guess.

The Americans were restless, as usual. One thing was very scarce among us at that time: patience. Everyone felt nervous and wanted things to happen. If it was time to get out, it was time to get out, before somebody changed their mind. Nevertheless, the only thing for us to do was wait for details of the surrender to be worked out and American forces to land.

Some of the guys went out in the countryside looking for those barrels of food, but most of us hung around camp, doing nothing but complaining now and then, and taking care of daily needs. There was no reading material, television, or radio, except the one the preacher had. All we heard from his radio was the war reports, so how to kill time was a big consideration.

Frustrated, Kirby, O'Brien, and I began talking about what to do. O'Brien, who'd been a camp black-market wheeler-dealer, said, "I'm flush with Philippine funny money. Let's find out if we can see Japan on it. We can listen to the radio on the way, and get back if it sounds like anything's up."

Kirby said, "I guess your money won't be any good in the States. We might as well use it up."

"Well, let's find a train," I said, and we hiked off to the main train station in town.

We had no hankering to go north, so we climbed aboard the first train going south on an odyssey I'll never forget. Japan is only about as large as the state of California, but with lots more people living there. The train was crowded. Soon, we were rolling south toward Tokyo. No one asked for a ticket, and we got a free ride.

The Japanese travelers were quiet and somber. They paid no attention to us. I guess their minds were full of the war, its tragic end at Hiroshima and Nagasaki, as well as the Tokyo area, and things they needed to do now. With the surrender, everything seemed up in the air for them as well as us. We rolled through carefully tended green farms and gardens on our way into the Tokyo area.

I shall never forget the sight of the city of Tokyo as we came in from the north. We had heard about the Allied fire bombing of certain cities, but I was not ready for that desolate landscape. We passed mile after mile of burned-out homes, with only a stone fence or chimney left to show where they'd stood. A few lucky souls' homes had survived the fires, but not many. People seemed to wander aimlessly past our train windows.

"Begorrah!" O'Brien said under his breath.

The firebombs had not destroyed the railroad, so train service continued as it always had. This was good, because the railroad served as Japan's main means of transportation. At any rate, we pulled into the Tokyo train station and almost everyone got off. It wasn't long before another train was ready to continue south. We knew enough Japanese to get from one to the other, and those people took to those funny-money American bills gladly. We could get whatever we needed with very little of that money.

Before long, we were traveling through Yokohama and on south. Yokohama was pretty well burned out also. I learned later that the Allies had burned out the city of Kawasaki, too. That took care of the three major cities making up the Tokyo Bay triangle. I couldn't imagine that many civilians killed, wounded, or left homeless. What pressure on the Japanese warlords and the Emperor! Not enough to move them to pity for their people, though.

The train made good time, and it wasn't long before

we entered the industrial city of Nagoya. The landscape there looked no different from that of the Tokyo Bay area. The civilian population of Japan had certainly taken a beating, but the warlords had been determined to hang on, and they made it worse, no doubt.

Next we came to another city burned out by the Allies, the industrial city of Osaka. When I recognized it, I said, "Kirby, this is where I first saw Japan. It was after the Hell ship, and I nearly died. If it hadn't been for this old Japanese doctor, I would have. He didn't have medicine, but he sure had a wake-up call. Set up a coffin for me in the corner. Fella, that'll get ya thinking."

Kirby didn't answer at first. He looked out the train window, and finally, softly, said, "I remember coming to Japan. Do you want to get off the train?"

"Nope. I remember Osaka too well as it is." How little I cared that it lay in ruin. I could not dredge up any pity for this place. This city had been the scene of too many painful events for me.

Kirby understood without my explaining anything. That was one thing about POWs—we knew each other's suffering, were comrades in it, through it, because of it.

I did not see the dry dock project I had worked on in 1943. I imagine the B-29s probably destroyed it.

"It was a camp called Tanagawa," I said. "It claimed a boy named Dale who shared my blanket." My eyes started to burn. Maybe that was a good sign.

From Osaka, we headed down the narrow portion of the main island of Japan. I was hoping we would be able to see the city of Hiroshima after it had been destroyed by that first atomic bomb, but for some reason, the train went around the city and down to the southern tip of

Honshu, the main island. Maybe the tracks had been destroyed in Hiroshima.

We did get to go on south to Nagasaki, where the second atomic bomb was dropped. Low mountains surround Nagasaki. We came over the mountain from the north. My breath caught in my chest. Sheer, utter waste stretched clear across the valley. Every building in the largely residential city had been blown flat. Their frame and clapboard houses, much like those on the Panhandle, had been blown to *nothing* for miles. The people we saw appeared shocked, digging aimlessly in the rubble. Some were bandaged, others just looked tattered and dirty. None were dressed protectively to avoid radiation, because no one knew the effects of radiation after a nuclear bomb blast. This was the first time atomic bombs had ever been exploded in a populated region. Nagasaki had also been an industrial city, but was now mile after mile of utter destruction.

The Allies had offered the same surrender opportunity after the fire-bombing of five major cities. The warlords and the Emperor refused. They refused again after the first atomic bomb on Hiroshima. This city, whose utter ruin we were seeing with our own eyes, lay destroyed for the same reason. It had taken even more—laying waste to the entire Tokyo area and, finally, the Akita Refinery Complex about 270 miles northwest of Tokyo, where all the oil for the whole country was refined and distributed—before the Emperor had instructed Hideki Tojo and his warlords to surrender.

We rode through the center of the valley of Nagasaki, three POWs watching history unfold, seeing what people now only read about in history books. Yes, there were shadows of people on buildings where they had stood when the bomb fell. She was a city much of whose population had turned to dust. Only on the outskirts was anything still standing.

I felt sad here.

I hated war and death all over again here.

I desperately wanted to go to my home, and comfort my loved ones.

As the train pulled out of Nagasaki, I thought about how we had assessed our options and then used what we had, to experience the trip of my lifetime. I never again expected to play a part in the making of history, or to see it unfolding before my eyes in this way.

At this point, we heard news reports saying the Allies nearly had their evacuation stations ready. It was time to head north, so we caught another train. After an uneventful trip, our train pulled into the main station at Tokyo. It was reassuring to see the newly arrived military policemen and Navy Shore Patrol on the platform. It was good to have healthy, well-fed Americans around again.

We were provided a truck ride to a processing center on the docks. I believe the town was Yokohama. There, in Tokyo Bay, were all those ships flying American flags. It seemed our preacher friend in camp's talk of a heavy involvement by the British fleet wasn't too visible.

We checked in, were given new clothes, and sent to the showers. Man, it was nice to take a nice, hot shower with plenty of soap, and don uniforms without a single hole. We then got our medical examinations. This is when I weighed in at ninety-eight pounds of skin and bones. That was my bottom weight. We traded our last funny money from the Philippines for Japanese yen. I had $4.65 left. It was worth a large stack of yen. The officials said we could spend the yen, but not American dollars.

Next, we were instructed to take a truck to a warehouse prepared as a residence for American POWs awaiting shipment to the US. At the loading area, we found an unusual situation: the foreign POWs were being sent directly to the airport to be flown out of Japan. Americans, on the other hand, were awaiting departure in the warehouse. For Kirby, O'Brien, and me, it was back to basics.

Our options included further cooling of our heels in this prison-like warehouse, or attempting to get to the airport and take our chances. The three of us chose option #2. We met a truck driver who had recently arrived in Japan.

"I've been instructed to haul POWs," he said.

"Great! How much yen do you need?" O'Brien asked.

"How much you got?" he answered.

We pooled our yen, gave it to him, and in a heartbeat we were on our way.

"Our ex-first lady, Eleanor Roosevelt, has been pressing Washington to quarantine all American POWs for six months to guard against communicable disease. You guys are smart to hurry on home," he told us, as we rumbled out on the field.

"What a 'Welcome Home' that would be," Kirby observed.

"Yeah, she's quite a piece of work, that woman."

He let us off at a large canteen at the Tokyo Airport. They were serving free coffee and donuts—some of those good things American POWs hadn't easily learned to do without. We thoroughly enjoyed our re-introduction to donuts.

Naturally, we were standouts in a crowd of American

service people and about twenty foreigners awaiting transportation.

"Man, you look as underfed as some of those Brits," one soldier observed.

"Ya'll been eatin' somewhat better'n us, I expect," I drawled.

"You a POW?"

"Yep, almost four years' worth."

"You from Texas?" an Air Force captain asked. "Sure sound like it. I'm from Lubbock, myself."

"I'm lookin' forward to gettin' back to the east side of Amarillo just as soon as we can catch a plane out of here," I replied.

"Well, hell, fella! I'm a pilot. I'm getting ready to fly a load of foreign POWs to Okinawa this evening. Why don't you and your buddies come along with me?"

"I believe Ms. Roosevelt wants to keep us under wraps for a bit."

"That's the dumbest damn stunt she's pulled lately. Your families have waited long enough!" he said, loudly.

"What did you have in mind?" I asked.

Indicating a camouflaged military Jeep sitting on the tarmac, he said, "Hop in that Jeep over there, and I'll show you."

The Road Leads Home
September–November 1945

OUT AT HIS AIRPLANE, THE PILOT EXPLAINED TO THE SUPERvisor of a group of POWs from the West Indies that he had three too many men on board. After a lot of yelling, three of them came off the plane, and we had room to climb on. We arrived in Okinawa late that night.

The first thing I saw was a sign on a Red Cross station that read Coca Cola. What an appetizer! Naturally, having gotten boxes in the camp and the coffee and donuts free in Japan, I expected the Coke to be free, too. However, this young lady wanted *fifty cents* for a Coke! Cokes had cost a nickel when I left home. I had to settle for free coffee and donuts again.

American soldiers, who asked questions and listened to our tales of POW life all the way, took us to a tent city where we bedded down. They told us to watch the bulletin board for a plane ride being arranged to Manila. However, the next day, the public address system blared that a large typhoon was headed our way. All aircraft prepared to fly out. The Navy put their ships out to sea to ride out the storm. That typhoon turned out to be one of the worst ever. We only stayed two days on Okinawa.

We caught a B-24 bomber going to Manila early in the morning. The pilot thought he could fly through the storm, but that proved impossible. The B-24 turned out all the power it could, but seemed to stand still. I believe every seam in that plane leaked, so we got wet.

The pilot turned around, flew over to the west, and around the storm. We soared over Corregidor and Manila Bay before we landed at the old Nichols Field. However, I did not get to see the Rock, as there were no portholes on the B-24s. We were taken to the 29th Replacement Center to the west of Nichols Field. We got bunks in Tent City, where we could wait for a plane to the States, but the wait wasn't long.

Early one morning a soldier woke us, saying we should return to Nichols Field to catch a plane to March Air Force Base in Southern California. I was ready for that.

We were walking across the tarmac when I noticed some soldiers checking the papers of guys in front of us. I had no papers. "Kirby, O'Brien," I whispered, "You got any papers?" I figured they had no papers, and they didn't. My last US papers were lost on Monkey Point.

"Orders," the lieutenant demanded.

I looked as bewildered as I could muster. "Sir, I've been a POW in Japan since 1942. My last papers were lost on Corregidor. I don't have any orders, sir."

The officer yelled, "Military police!" never taking his eyes from us. He had no way of knowing whether we were legitimate or not.

They hauled all of us back to the 29th Replacement

Center, where I was questioned alone. I didn't see Kirby or O'Brien ever again. I guess the brass wanted to hear our stories separately. The military turned me over to the Federal Bureau of Investigation (FBI) for debriefing. Their interrogation lasted about another week or ten days.

There was no Central Intelligence Agency at that time, and the FBI carried out all investigations. The relationship I began with them that day lasted about three years, as they investigated and prosecuted those 5,700 B- and C-class criminals who were caught and brought to trial. From what I gather, about 3,000 were convicted. These included my two favorites of the whole bunch—the Japanese-American traitor from San Francisco, the one I call Hangnecker, and my other favorite, that mean Japanese supervisor at the mine, Rabbit Ass. Hangnecker got the death penalty. Rabbit Ass' nickname got him caught. He was tried and sentenced to prison.

While I was at 29th Replacement Center, I had a thorough physical examination that found I had a piece of shrapnel in my back, beriberi, and some kind of amoeba thing. My papers were brought up to date, and I received a partial payday. It was not bad around there. I revisited Manila, and saw how the Japanese had trashed the place before US Forces defeated them. I also returned to Niac, where we'd blown up the Japanese long gun. The gun had disappeared, but the old church building was still a wreck. I never returned to Corregidor. It wasn't being encouraged at that time. I would have liked to.

When I left the 29th Replacement Center, I was not exercising my options. Therefore, my transportation to the US was arranged for me. At the docks in Manila, a large, white ship with a Red Cross painted on it waited for me.

Aboard, I found a nice clean bunk with white sheets, in an airy compartment where other returning POWs and I enjoyed getting to know each other. Soon, we sailed for San Francisco. What a switch from the last time I left Manila aboard that Hell ship!

I met Dr. M.C. Overton, Jr. on that hospital ship. He was a fine doctor. He put me into the weight-gaining business while we crossed the Pacific.

The first time I talked to him, he said, "Baker, you're looking a little thin," grinning. "Now, I know you can't cram in a cheeseburger, fries, and a strawberry shake right off. Your stomach has shrunk. So what we'll do is push it for a few more goodies each time." He clapped me on the back and handed me a cookie.

I followed his plan, and by the time we sighted California, in about twenty-five days, I was eating pretty normally. He also began work on my amoebic dysentery and Beriberi.

"The shrapnel in your back," he said, "will have to wait until we've got better facilities to check you out."

We sailed into the US underneath the Golden Gate Bridge, sometime in the first part of October 1945. What a sight! Those golden mountains—dotted with live oak trees coming down to the water on one side of the arched bridge—contrasted with that teeming city on the other, while underneath, the waters of San Francisco Bay rolled in to North America.

After five years, in spite of serious doubts here and there on my part, I was coming home. All those able were permitted on deck to see the passage under the bridge. POWs wept and saluted and clapped each other on the back. I put my hand over my heart, because there was no dirt at hand to kiss. Once we'd had a glimpse of Angel Island again, all passengers returned to our beds.

We were not permitted to see our ship dock, or to haul our duffle bags down the gangplank. Each of us had to wait on porters to help us off. As I followed mine, I could hear the cheers of a welcoming crowd before I even left the bulkhead. Some had come to meet their loved ones returning home, but there were a lot of happy Americans on that dock. It appeared that some of them just came to welcome "the boys" home.

"Hey soldier, thanks for a job well done. You are all our heroes," one young woman, wearing a blue dress and carrying a baby, said to me.

I smiled at her. "A job well done" was what we'd accomplished, I guessed. But a hero? When you do what is right—fight for your country's freedom when you are called to—does *that* make you a hero? I didn't feel much like a hero. I guess I didn't feel much of anything, except glad to be back on US soil.

The soldiers from the Red Cross ship rode green army buses to Letterman General Hospital in the Presidio Military Reservation of San Francisco, which is directly across the bay from Angel Island. At Letterman, we ate four meals per day with a snack in between if we wanted it. If we wanted food, all we had to do was ask, and during the week or so we were there, we began to put on weight quickly. I asked for pork chops, mashed potatoes, and gravy several times.

Since my mother and dad couldn't afford a phone in their home, I sent Mom a Western Union telegram telling her I was back on American soil and would be home soon.

The City of San Francisco went out of their way to accommodate us. We were given the group key to that city.

Most of those in the food and service industries provided free food and service, as long as we were in our hospital clothes, pajamas, and robes.

Bob Hope and Bing Crosby came by the hospital to put on their show. Their antics and laughter were in stark contrast to what we'd lived with all through our POW time, and I could feel my spirit beginning to awake as they performed. I glanced around at the other guys during that show, and saw only half-smiles on most of the faces. I guess we all thought this reality was a 180-degree turn from the reality we'd recently experienced.

We were also invited to attend a Lawrence Welk show at the Mark Hopkins Hotel. I loved it—even the bubbles. There were professional sports events to attend—baseball and football games. That city knew how to welcome the boys home. The United Nations was being formed, and we read about it in the *San Francisco Chronicle*, also provided free. They had what was called Fleet Week on San Francisco Bay, for which we had front row seats at the Presidio. We truly enjoyed our short stay in the City by the Bay, but even so, most of us longed to finish our trips home.

Then, one morning, the POWs and wounded from Texas boarded more green buses, rode to an Air Force base north of the city, and flew to Brooke General Hospital in San Antonio, Texas. At last, I was checked out. I got a thirty-day furlough to visit home. When I walked out the double front doors of that hospital, I bent over and picked up a handful of that Texas dirt. I looked at that wonderful stuff, and tears ran down my face, turning it into Texas mud.

At the Greyhound station, as soon as I got my bus schedule, I sent my mom another telegram to let her know when I would be getting home. There were men in uniform all over the station that day. The war was over, and everyone hurried to go home as fast as possible. I joined the crowd at Gate 10 as soon as they announced the bus for McLean over the loudspeaker. A little lady struggled up near me, dragging a suitcase that looked as if it weighed twice as much as she did. Her gray hair was twisted up into a bun at the nape of her neck, just like my mother did her hair. A couple of soldiers and a woman in high heels elbowed in front of her, headed for the bus.

"Hold it, lady," the driver said to the woman in heels. She tried to push past him, but he was firm. "Military go first!" Another soldier walked up next to the little woman who reminded me of Mom. I caught his eye, and glanced down at her.

The soldier looked down at her and said, "How do you do, Maam?"

"Right nicely, thank you," she answered. She even sounded kind of like Mom.

I offered her my arm, and she took it. He offered his, and grabbed her suitcase. We ushered her right past the woman in heels, up to the bus driver, and as my new friend handed him the suitcase, I said, "This is our mother." On the bus we went. I never even knew where she was going.

During that long, slow bus trip, clear across the largest state in the union to the top of Texas, where my family waited, I spent the time thinking about my life. I considered who I had become, for I had changed. I wasn't as thin now as when I'd first left Japan, but my physical condition would never be the same. The physical side of things wasn't all that had changed, though.

The nurses had discovered that they couldn't touch me

when I was asleep—I'd wake up swinging. The world of the POW was gone in my waking hours, but in my dreams it was still quite real. My emotions were shot. I had practiced not letting anything overwhelm me for a long time, no matter how evil or horrible. Now it was hard to care about some things. Thinking about that made me wonder if those three POWs we'd bumped in Okinawa were nearly home now. At any rate, I wanted to just be left alone, find peace wherever it might be. I thought the best way to do that was to do whatever else the Army required of me, and avoid being noticed.

Perhaps the only thing about me that was stronger was my faith in God. After all, here I was, headed home, when the odds had certainly been against it. Riding back through the prairies of Amarillo that afternoon, my mind was racing, but my hope transplant was intact. I wondered what I would find when I got to that small town on Route 66, where I had caught a ride with the paper man at two a.m. nearly five years ago.

I'd found a seat next to an old soldier headed for a little town near McLean. He struck up a conversation with me, and I told him I wondered whether my folks had changed as much as I had. "Do you think we'll still know each other, still connect?" I asked him.

"Son, war is hell and love is amazing. You had love before the war, and I'll bet you'll have it like you never left as soon as they see you. That's how it's worked for me."

"I'm worried," I answered. "Maybe it's not about them. Maybe it's about me. In one moment, I know I need them, and will this bus to roll faster, and then in the next moment, I worry they won't be able to deal with all that I've become. I'm physically sick. My legs are shot from being frozen. And sometimes I just go numb, and don't even want to think about anything."

"Just get off the bus, boy," he said, as we rolled past the first house in McLean. I'd left in the early morning. Today, I was returning as the sun was setting.

A wisp of a lady who never weighed over 100 pounds in her life stood on the curb waiting for me. She stood proudly in front of about 2,000 people behind her and Dad, who watched to see that mother's son return to her. Mom was a Gold-Star Mother, who had three stars standing for three sons away at war posted on her front door. The town waited to help her welcome home one of those sons whom the Army had wanted to write off, but whose mother wouldn't hear of it.

Mom told me later that the Army had desired to change my status from MIA (missing in action) to KIA (killed in action). They would have had an honorary funeral and would have paid my insurance. However, her hope and faith were in good shape as always, and she refused to have anything to do with that. She also said that during the first week of August 1945, she received one of my "Good News" cards written from Japan. The other 168 had never been mailed. When that one reached the McLean post office, the postmaster grabbed it and ran four blocks to Mom's house. Thus, the whole town had heard the good news.

An eternity ended as the bus driver announced, "McLean, Texas," opened the door, and stepped down to the pavement. Nobody in the bus stood up. They could see her waiting, and they gave me the honor of being first off the bus. As my feet hit the blacktop, my little sister's body and open arms hit me full force. She could only hug me and cry as we walked toward the curb where Mom stood.

Mom and I went into a full embrace with not a word spoken. My mother's love for her son who had been lost, but now was found, was all I felt, all I needed. Dad put his hand on my shoulder and his other arm around Mom, smiling. The townspeople were all yelling, "Welcome home," but inside the love of my family, all I heard was *home*.

It was my mom who finally broke the silence of our embrace, with, "Let's go home, son. Your supper is getting cold."

After War
Epilogue

AFTER FIFTY-EIGHT YEARS OF LIVING WITH MEMORIES AND researching the subject of World War II in the South Pacific, I've learned some truth about life that I think might help others.

Beginning with the end, I believe the most graphic description of that valley of Nagasaki after the bomb has been painted by a Japanese artist named Fujita. The bombed-out city of Nagasaki seemed to be etched in his mind forever when he painted the full skeleton of a man riding the full skeleton of a horse with sword drawn, grinning fiendishly as he rides through that valley strewn with dry human bones. The background of his painting is colored in the chlorine-like green of death. Fujita's painting depicts the horror of Nagasaki, and also of war itself. War is hell, and I am glad that one is over.

If you have wondered why so many relatively healthy US Army soldiers died during that Bataan Death March, on Corregidor, soon after arriving at POW Camp

O'Donnell, or at one of the Cabanatuan POW Camps, or at a camp in Japan, there is an answer. It is true that hundreds, then thousands, died in a very short time. Ask yourself how long it takes for the atrocious, horrendous, uncivilized treatment of an ungodly enemy to kill those they have under their control.

You may also wonder why some died and some lived. Perhaps circumstance, the luck of the draw, or hope vs. the lack of it could be the answers. This life promises us nothing, whether we do right or wrong. Our only hope is in God—not that He will give us the life we wish for, but that He is God, He does love us, and there is Heaven for those who trust Him.

What I know of the fate of the other men I served and labored with is this. The preacher went home with the British personnel. Kirby became a successful businessman in the Midwest. Johnnie went to a VA facility in the Midwest. Colonel Can Do became commander of a university ROTC training center. I know this because he sent an Army recruiter to try to get me to re-enlist. Joe returned to New York. Casey was lost in a refinery fire in Japan. Hard Nose got to Brooke General Hospital; after that, I don't know what happened to him. Dewey got home, but he moved to Oklahoma and I didn't see him much. I've already spoken of those brave men who gave their lives on Corregidor or in Japan. About the rest, I have no information.

I discovered, upon my return home, that the florist in McLean had sent flowers and candy to my mother every Mother's Day while I was a POW, without request or payment. It is the small kindnesses, the service we do without expectation of return, that make this life worth living. War is hell partly because it takes these away.

On December 8, 1945, I married a very beautiful young lady named Neva. She has become the love of my life and the mother of my three children. She lived with me through the times I fought the demons of POW life in Japan each night and struggled to return to normal living during the days. I can never thank her enough for that.

On June 9, 1946, I was discharged, as a corporal, from the Army at Brooke General Hospital, San Antonio, Texas. June 10 of the same year, I was placed on the medical rolls of the Veterans Administration (VA), with 100-percent disability compensation. The pay was set at $115 per month, and that was not enough to support my family.

Therefore, I went to accounting school and gave up a large percentage of my compensation in order to work for a large corporation. I soon became a supervisor in the accounting department and could support my family.

My health has never returned to good condition, but I've learned to live with flashbacks, amoeba, Beriberi, leg and back pain, ace bandages, pain pills, support hose, knee braces, a back brace, etc. That little piece of shrapnel lodged near a vertebra in my back is inoperable, and manages to remind me of Monkey Point every chance it gets.

Our good Dr. Overton, as well as those doctors and nurses at the VA, have always been top-of-the-line. Dr. Overton remained my doctor for about twenty years, because he opened a practice in Pampa, Texas, where I lived. I appreciate all the VA doctors and nurses have done for me over the more than fifty years since World War II ended.

In 1963, I was chosen of God to pursue a career in the pastoral ministry. Serving the people of God was rewarding until 1978, when my health dropped to a new low. During 1978, problems with my kidneys, prostate, equilibrium—

along with all the other medical problems I've mentioned—kicked in with a vengeance. I spent a lot of time at the VA hospital. We began a long, tough fight to convince the government that my time in POW camp had caused these continuing health problems, and we struggled through miles of administrative red tape. The government finally placed me back on 100-percent disability compensation.

But back to beginning at the end, an interesting thing happened to me about forty years after the war. A Japanese grandmother came to see me at my church in Vacaville, California. Her name was Akie Fuller. She was visiting her daughter and grandchild, who were then stationed at Travis Air Force Base. Akie had lived in Nagasaki when we dropped the bomb. She told me her memory of the eleven a.m. bombing of that valley of desolation at Nagasaki on August 9, 1945.

She had been seven years old, and saw the flash of light through her kitchen window. She felt the shock waves as they knocked her house around when the concussion spread. Her family lived far on the outskirts of the city, so there was no fire or full destruction of her home. Her people had no idea what had happened to them. Some of her family members received injuries, and had to move into a public shelter. Her family life was changed forever.

It was a Sunday morning in 1988 when this grandmother and her daughter visited me in the worship service of Faith Baptist Church. We enjoyed sharing what we knew of the war with each other, and hearing that she had survived helped me. She copied her notes of my sermon in Japanese and gave them to me as a souvenir of our meeting. There was no animosity. We both knew that people in wartime become part of something larger than they are.

At any rate, Akie had grown to adulthood, met a young man, married, and a daughter was born to this young family. Somewhere along life's road, Akie had learned about Jesus and trusted Him as her personal Savior.

Her daughter grew to adulthood, and met and married an American serviceman. They were transferred to Travis Air Force Base in California, where their baby was born. Naturally, Grandmother Akie visited.

I had been honored at the base with a bronze star. This received a write-up in the local newspaper. Akie made the connection and came to church where she met me. We had a nice visit—maybe God's way of salving wounds for both of us.

The burden of my heart for a long time has been the development of a vaccine for radiation to combat cancer cells in people before they become active. I know there is a lot of rebellion against any sort of radiation. However, that day in Vacaville, two people had experienced the worst kind of radiation. Two people who were grandparents, who had raised our families, while neither of us has had any cancer.

Therefore, it is my prayer and hope above all hope that someday our researchers can find the correct amount of radiation to apply to the human body to counteract cancer cells before they become active. It seems possible to me, because radiation is what doctors use to combat fully active cancer cells.

Like I have said before, war is hell. The flashbacks and pains of Hell don't go away, so I have learned to live with my condition. My good wife still provides a lot of support. I still like to "assess my options, then use what I have." It works.

I wish the United States would reconsider the stand we took following World War II about the compensation of Japanese POWs. I know there are considerations of countries recovering, but when Canadian, British, Dutch, Australian, New Zealand, and Norwegian governments allow compensation of their POWs, then there is also the consideration of justice. I also believe that Mitsui and other Japanese corporations making money in the United States should be charged to negotiate a settlement fund.

After a heart attack, stroke, and learning to walk with a walker, I still have Jesus in my heart. My hope transplant is still intact, and I hate to even think about anything except a positive attitude. Even though the flashbacks and pains of Hell will not go away, the power of this can never conquer the power of God.

God bless America is my prayer—because there is no better place on earth to live.

THE UNITED STATES OF AMERICA

TO ALL WHO SHALL SEE THESE PRESENTS, GREETING: THIS IS TO CERTIFY THAT THE PRESIDENT OF THE UNITED STATES OF AMERICA AUTHORIZED BY EXECUTIVE ORDER, 24 AUGUST 1962 HAS AWARDED

THE BRONZE STAR MEDAL

TO CORPORAL ARTHUR B. BAKER UNITED STATES ARMY

FOR meritorious achievement during combat while serving in the Southwest Pacific Theater of Operations from 7 December 1941 to 10 May 1942. The actions of Corporal Baker were in keeping with the highest traditions of the military service and reflect distinct credit upon him, his unit and the United States Army.

GIVEN UNDER MY HAND IN THE CITY OF WASHINGTON
THIS 3rd DAY OF September 1992

THE ADJUTANT GENERAL

SECRETARY OF THE ARMY

GENERAL HEADQUARTERS
ARMED FORCES OF THE PHILIPPINES
Camp General Emilio Aguinaldo
Quezon City, Philippines

CERTIFICATE OF AWARD

In recognition of the Military services of

Arthur Baker

during World War II, and pursuant to Armed Forces of the Philippines Regulations G 131-053, dated July 1, 1986, he is awarded and authorized to wear the

PHILIPPINE LIBERATION MEDAL
PHILIPPINE REPUBLIC PRESIDENTIAL UNIT CITATION BADGE
ASIATIC PACIFIC CAMPAIGN MEDAL
WORLD WAR II VICTORY MEDAL

Given this 23rd day of March 2000
at the Embassy of the Philippines
1600 Massachusetts Avenue, N.W.
Washington, D.C. 20036

By Order of the Chief of Staff, Armed Forces of the Philippines:

BONIFACIO B. RAMOS
Colonel PA (GSC)
Defense Attache

Tetsuji Kondoh
President of Denki Kagaku
Kogyo Co., Ltd.,
#3, 1-chome, Shintomi-cho,
Chuo-ku, Tokyo

July 31, 1947

Baker Arthur
General Delivery,
Mclean, Texas,
U. S. A.

My dear sir;

Two years have passed since I bid farewell at Aomi station.

I beg to pay my highest esteem and courtesy for your hard work while you were at Aomi for a long time & at the same time. I am anxious to know about your welfare since then.

We Japanese are endeavouring to bring about a spiritual revolution in speeding the establishment of a democratic, peaceloving & cultural nation.

I trust Japan will become a comfortable land in the near future and I hope you will have a good chance to visit Japan to inspect her old customs & manners.

Please give my best regards to your family

Believe me,

Yours sincerely.

T. Kondoh

CPL ARTHUR B. BAKER 18036274

To you who answered the call of your country and served in its Armed Forces to bring about the total defeat of the enemy, I extend the heartfelt thanks of a grateful Nation. As one of the Nation's finest, you undertook the most severe task one can be called upon to perform. Because you demonstrated the fortitude, resourcefulness and calm judgment necessary to carry out that task, we now look to you for leadership and example in further exalting our country in peace.

Harry Truman

THE WHITE HOUSE

Army of the United States

Honorable Discharge

THIS IS TO CERTIFY That Arthur B. Baker 18 036 274 Corporal 60th Coast Artillery Corregidor ARMY OF THE UNITED STATES, is hereby Honorably Discharged from the military service of the United States of America.

This certificate is awarded as a testimonial of Honest and Faithful Service to this country.

Given at Separation Center Fort Sam Houston, Texas

Date 9 June 1946

L. L. Stewart

Major AGD

ENLISTED RECORD AND REPORT OF SEPARATION
HONORABLE DISCHARGE

ERS

1. LAST NAME - FIRST NAME - MIDDLE INITIAL: Baker Arthur B.
2. ARMY SERIAL NO.: 18 036 274
3. GRADE: Cpl
4. ARM OR SERVICE: CA
5. COMPONENT: RA
6. ORGANIZATION: 60th Coast Artillery Corregidor
7. DATE OF SEPARATION: 9 June 46
8. PLACE OF SEPARATION: Separation Cente Fort Sam Houston Texas
9. PERMANENT ADDRESS FOR MAILING PURPOSES: Box 367 McLean Gray County Texas
10. DATE OF BIRTH: 16 Jan 18
11. PLACE OF BIRTH: Denton Texas
12. ADDRESS FROM WHICH EMPLOYMENT WILL BE SOUGHT: See 9
13. Color Eyes: blue
14. Color Hair: blonde
15. Height: 6' 0"
16. Weight: 156 lbs.
17. No. Depend.: 1
18. RACE: White X | Negro | Other (specify)
19. MARITAL STATUS: Single | Married X | Other (specify)
20. U.S. CITIZEN: Yes X | No
21. CIVILIAN OCCUPATION AND NO.: Salesman Petroleum Products 1-86.61

MILITARY HISTORY

22. DATE OF INDUCTION:
23. DATE OF ENLISTMENT: 3 Feb 41
24. Date of Entry into Active Service: 3 Feb 41
25. PLACE OF ENTRY INTO SERVICE: Rctg Sta Amarillo, Texas

Selective Service Data:
26. Registered: Yes X | No
27. Local S.S. Board No.: 1
28. COUNTY AND STATE: Gray County Texas
29. HOME ADDRESS AT TIME OF ENTRY INTO SERVICE: See 9
30. MILITARY OCCUPATIONAL SPECIALTY AND NO.: Truct Driver Heavy 931
31. Military Qualification and Date (i.e., infantry, aviation and marksmanship badges, etc.): none
32. BATTLES AND CAMPAIGNS: Philippine Islands Anti-Submarine GO 105 WD 45
33. DECORATIONS AND CITATIONS: American Defense Service Ribbon with 1 bronze star; Asiatic Pacific Campaign Ribbon with 2 bronze stars; Philippine Defense Service Ribbon with 1 bronze star; Good Conduct Medal; Distinguished #(see 55)
34. WOUNDS RECEIVED IN ACTION: None

35. LATEST IMMUNIZATION DATES

SMALLPOX	TYPHOID	TETANUS	OTHER (specify)
12Sep45	12Sep45	Unk	12Sep45-Cholera

36. SERVICE OUTSIDE CONTINENTAL U.S. AND RETURN

DATE OF DEPARTURE	DESTINATION	DATE OF ARRIVAL
1 Apr 41	AP	22 Apr 41
19 Sep 45	US	8 Oct 45

37. TOTAL LENGTH OF SERVICE

Continental Service Years	Months	Days	Foreign Service Years	Months	Days
0	9	29	4	6	8

38. HIGHEST GRADE HELD: Cpl
39. PRIOR SERVICE: none
40. REASON AND AUTHORITY FOR SEPARATION: Convenience of the Government (RR 1-1 Demobilization) AR 615-365 15Dec44
41. SERVICE SCHOOLS ATTENDED: Transportatin and Instrument
42. EDUCATION (Years): Grammar 8 | High Schl. 3 | College 0

PAY DATA Vou 5308

43. Longevity for Pay Purposes: Years	Months	Days	44. Mustering Out Pay: Total	This Payment	45. Soldier Deposits	46. Travel Pay	47. TOTAL AMOUNT, NAME OF DISBURSING OFFICER
5	4	7	$ 300	$ 100	90.00	$ 26.40	$302.53 B Jeffrey Lt Col FD

INSURANCE NOTICE

IMPORTANT IF PREMIUM IS NOT PAID WHEN DUE OR WITHIN THIRTY-ONE DAYS THEREAFTER, INSURANCE WILL LAPSE. MAKE CHECKS OR MONEY ORDERS PAYABLE TO THE TREASURER OF THE U. S. AND FORWARD TO COLLECTIONS SUBDIVISION, VETERANS ADMINISTRATION, WASHINGTON 25, D. C.

48. KIND OF INSURANCE: Nat. Serv.	U.S. Govt.	None	49. HOW PAID: Allotment	Direct to V.A.	50. Effective Date of Allotment Discontinuance	51. Date of Next Premium Due (One month after 50)	52. PREMIUM DUE EACH MONTH	53. INTENTION OF VETERAN TO: Continue	Continue Only $	Discontinue
X			X		30 June 46	31 Jul 46	$1.98	X		

54. RIGHT THUMB PRINT: Print

55. REMARKS (This space for completion of above items or entry of other items specified in W. D. Directives)
Lapel button issued
ASR Score (2 Sep 45) 96
Separated from the service on a partial service record and affadivit from the soldier.
#Unit Badge with 2 Oak Leaf Clusters GO 14 WD 9 March 42; Victory Ribbon; 1 Service Stripe; 7 Overseas Service Bars

56. SIGNATURE OF PERSON BEING SEPARATED: Arthur B. Baker

57. PERSONNEL OFFICER (Type name, grade and organization - signature): M. L. Clifton CWO USA Ass't Mil Pers Officer

Bibliography

Costello, John. *Pacific War 1941-1945* (Quill: New York, 1982). This is a history of World War II in the Pacific, very useful for the events of the war happening while POWs were being captured and living out their lives in captivity.

Daws, Gavan. *Prisoners of the Japanese: POWs of World War II in the Pacific* (New York: William Morrow and Co., Inc., 1994). Daws comprehensively covers the entire zone of captivity of the Japanese in the Pacific. His work is indexed and includes pictures.

Goetz Holmes, Linda. *Unjust Enrichment* (Mechanicsburg, PA: Stackpole Books, 2001). Goetz Holmes is the first Pacific War historian appointed to the US Government Interagency Working Group, which locates and declassifies material about World War II war crimes. She has interviewed more than 400 ex-POWs. Her book is the explanation of her research about how Japan's companies built postwar fortunes using American POWs.

Kerr, E. Bartlett. *Surrender and Survival: the Experience of American POWs in the Pacific, 1941-1945* (New York: William Morrow and Co., Inc., 1985). A book written by the son of a POW on the subject of POWs from the many Pacific fronts. It covers the 1944 and 1945 arrivals of POWs in Japan.

Knox, Donald and Falk, Stanley. *Death March: The Survivors of Bataan*. Knox talked to sixty-eight survivors of the Death March, and compiled their stories of camps in the Philippines and Japan.

Pearson, Judith L. *Belly of the Beast* (New York: New American Library, Penguin Putnam Inc., 1953). This book was written posthumously about the experience of Navy medic and POW Estel Myers, aboard several Hell ships.

Sides, Hampton. *Ghost Soldiers: The Forgotten Epic Story of World War II's Most Dramatic Mission* (New York: Doubleday, Division of Random House, Inc. 2001). Sides tells the story of the liberation of Cabanatuan POW camps in the Philippines.

Tenney, Lester and Stockdale, James. *My Hitch in Hell: the Bataan Death March* (Washington: Brassey's, 1995). *My Hitch in Hell* is another book that covers the surrender of Bataan and POW camps in the Philippines.

Wright, John, M. Jr. *Captured on Corregidor: Diary of an American POW in World War II* (Jefferson, NC: McFarland and Co., Inc. Publishers). Wright tells the story of his capture, time interned in a Philippine POW camp, and transfer in 1945 to a Japanese POW camp.